For the sky and the earth, wind and rain of this ancient beautiful land we have the privilege to work and live upon, in particular the Gadigal and Wangal people of the Eora Nation on whose land our sites dwell. We acknowledge and pay our respects to elders - past, present and emerging.

Egg of the Universe

SEASONAL EATING • MOVEMENT AND MEDITATION
NOURISHING MEALS • PROBIOTIC FERMENTS • DELICIOUS TREATS

Egg of the Universe

RECIPES FOR LIFE FROM
THE WHOLEFOODS CAFÉ
AND YOGA STUDIO

BRYONY & HARRY LANCASTER

murdoch books
Sydney | London

Contents

WARNING: YOGA AND WHOLEFOODS HAVE BEEN KNOWN TO CAUSE HEALTH AND HAPPINESS

Introduction

We remember the day we dreamt up Egg of the Universe. We were sitting in our little flat in London, gazing out a window overlooking the park. We imagined a place where we could combine our passions of yoga and good food, a place where you could go for a yoga class then enjoy a nourishing meal afterwards, where you felt a sense of genuine community and could practise the art of combining modern science and ancient wisdom in a lighthearted and fun way.

We were both very young when we first met, just 22 and 23 years old. At the time we weren't at all into pickling vegetables, eating seasonally, yoga or self-development. We were more interested in the next great dance party or debaucherous dinner with friends. But we were then – and still are – seekers, searching for that elusive inner peace, expansiveness and, ultimately, freedom. This pursuit led us from the dance floors of London to yoga and meditation and, eventually, to the opening of our studios and cafés in Sydney. After 15 years filled with many ups and downs – from moments of pure celebration and clarity, to nights when we couldn't sleep because of the pressure – we've succeeded in creating what we dreamed up all those years ago.

What's kept us going, and what keeps us getting out of bed each day, is both the enjoyment of what we do and a real sense of purpose. We continue to be inspired by seeing happy people enjoying lunch in the sun or learning how to pickle their veggies in one of our workshops, and watching the daily transformations of our students as they grow and find more freedom through yoga and meditation. We genuinely feel delight in having centres like ours in the world where people can connect, laugh and heal, so that healing can spread into our families, workplaces and wider communities.

We want to help make the world a better place, one person at a time. But we also believe wholeheartedly that the greatest transformation needs to begin with us. Everything that we offer at Egg of the Universe is an extension of what we practise at home. From the way we eat, to the practices we teach, we aim (not always successfully) to take what we learn on the yoga mat into our lives, in the way we parent and run our business, and how we are with each other in our relationship. The idea for us is to live a more grounded life – one full of joy and celebration in everyday moments, and which harnesses tools to navigate the more challenging terrain that's present in any modern life.

The intention behind this book is to provide more tools for finding better balance and to put some pillars in place for you so life feels more enjoyable, healthy and fun. Health and wellness for us isn't just one thing, and there are no shortcuts. In our experience, it's more like having many spokes on the wheel.

Our pillars: yoga and wholefoods

Yoga and wholefoods, as practices, are slow medicine. It takes time, patience and dedication to bring the seeds of these practices to fruition. But they do work, and have done for many thousands of years, for millions of people before us. There is a Sanskrit word, 'patheya', that means 'provisions for a journey'. That's what we feel this book is for: to deliver provisions for a life that enables a deeper connection to the world around and within us. A life in which we can be tuned into the changing seasons, combining the elements of movement, breath and meditation along with nourishing wholefoods to help us feel more grounded.

Often we think of yoga as just bendy bodies and stretchy pants, but at its core it's about following an invitation of systematised practice to move from distraction and separation towards nirvana, or Samadhi. Nirvana aside, yoga is said to improve sleep, decrease levels of the stress hormone cortisol in our body, and increase flexibility, muscle tone and, ultimately, happiness – no wonder it's becoming so popular! For many people, yoga is also a way to manage anxiety and depression, as well as to help carve out a path towards meditation. Above all, though, and especially for us, yoga is a way of feeling part of something bigger than ourselves.

The word 'yoga' is often translated as 'union' or 'to yoke'. We see it as a means to bring together all the fractured parts of our body, mind and heart so that we feel more complete within ourselves. Yoga is an opportunity to strengthen and heal through physical postures, breathing, contemplation and self-reflection. Not only does yoga help us feel stronger and more balanced, but it can also remedy much of the discord within us and help with how we relate to the world around us. With practice and time, everyday life can become more illuminated, leading to more lasting contentment and holistic health. While yoga is an age-old practice, spanning different continents and cultures, it feels more relevant today than ever before.

At Egg of the Universe we try to bring that same philosophy into how we share and consume food – listening to our bodies and moving with the flow of the seasons, bringing that sense of strength and balance into the everyday practice of eating, with an emphasis on wholefoods, nutrition and mindfulness.

As far back as we can remember, we've been passionate about good food. In this book, we'd love to share with you what wholefoods are and the basic principles of how you can implement mindfulness practices into your eating for total wellbeing. Simply put, this book will empower you to discover your own internal nutritional compass; to help you lead a life filled with a style of cooking and diet that is both satisfying and nutritious. Ultimately, our dream is for this book to be a guiding force in helping to reclaim common-sense principles when it comes to the growing, preparing and eating of good food.

For us, this book is a way to stretch our arms a little wider to encourage you to follow a framework of seasonally inspired recipes and practices. To connect more deeply with the changing seasons, while noticing more about your inner world, and in doing so, developing more self-awareness and tools for grounding yourself. It's also about tuning in, and allowing ourselves (even as city dwellers) to connect to the earth's cycles and to use the messages from nature to guide our choices about how and what we eat.

More than anything, this book is intended to be a practical guide through the seasons for nutrition, movement and stillness. A guide to living aimed to enhance your awareness of yourself, and of what feels good for you and your body throughout the year.

The best way to start this journey is to explore this book for yourself. Be your own guide, play around with the ideas offered here, look at the concepts raised, make the recipes and notice how they make you feel. If the end results are positive, then share that new-found knowledge through a joyful celebration of good food. Let the ripple effect begin.

Thank you for reading our book. We hope it brings enjoyment of and connection to the food you eat and the way you move through each season.

Love,

Bryony and Harry xx

MY YOGA JOURNEY

I began to practise yoga when I was working in television and film production, squeezing in morning sessions before gruelling 12-hour shifts. My days were fuelled by adrenaline and stress, and I sustained myself with cups of coffee and panic – often I'd sit bolt upright in the middle of the night, having forgotten to do something really important, such as order enough film for the crew or update the call time for the lead actor. Very soon my 6am yoga class became the best part of every day, before the chaos of life began.

I was interested in the way I'd feel after class – stable and grounded, with a deep sense of peace and wellbeing, not just in my physical body, but also my inner world. I may not have been able to articulate it then, but for the first time in my adult life, I glimpsed a spaciousness beyond my ordinary mind, and that alone was enough to keep me coming back.

I've never been overly interested in becoming super flexible, mastering intricate postures or getting 'yoga buff'. For me, the gift of yoga quickly became a tool for inner freedom. A way of tending to my inner restlessness. Of course, I am grateful for feeling stronger and more flexible, calmer and more grounded, but I am less interested in my body looking a certain way than using it as a gateway to feeling better within myself.

Yoga has taken me from a place where I felt disconnected and fractured to feeling many more moments of peace throughout the day. What started as a practice for my body slowly became a way of life and continues to offer opportunities for transformation and growth.

As a mother of two, partner to a man I have loved for more than 20 years and a business owner, life can feel very full and very fast. I know the challenge is one shared by many working parents. The pace of life picks up for us after the quiet of our morning practice. As Harry cooks the kids' breakfast, I make sure they've completed their homework and have clean clothes to wear. Harry arranges their school lunchboxes, I ensure they have their musical instruments or soccer/swimming/football kit for the day. Harry and I work as a team, both at home and within the business, to direct and lead the yoga studios and cafés, which can be both inspiring and challenging, and requires us to bring deep awareness to how we are together. It's a juggle, and striking a balance between *keeping the home and family united and nourished while managing the responsibilities for the business and its vision can be difficult. Add all the mundane details that fill up our home life, and it often feels nothing short of overwhelming.*

I've found that balancing the movement of yoga and the stillness of meditation is the most potent remedy for my life. I practise to uncoil the tightness in my body, to unravel some of the tension, to feed energy back through the corridors of my body and to bring me out of my head and back home again, whole again within myself. To have the space and time to tend to and befriend the fractured parts of me and to feel grounded once more. From that place, I can go out into the world and share what I love to do.

Finding your practice

Do not mistake the finger pointing for the moon.

– GAUTAMA BUDDHA FROM THE SURANGAMA SUTRA

This quote captures so much of the practice for me and the world of yoga. If we spend too much time worrying about the intricacies of the method – which yoga style is better, the details of our practice, the name of our teacher, the exact details of how the physical posture ought to be expressed, whether the room should be heated or music on or off – we are getting stuck on the limitation of the description of yoga, the finger pointing at the moon, rather than basking in the magnificence of moonlight itself. Yoga ultimately must be experienced to be understood. It's important not to get caught up and fixated on the mental constructs and the methods of yoga, but to look to the light of the moon and to feel within your body its potential and beauty, and ultimately to know this as you!

Yoga at Egg of the Universe

Like everything at Egg, what we offer is an extension of what we practise at home, what feels best for us. It has changed over the years, as we have, and it will continue to change with us. What we share through Egg feels like the most balanced and transformative combination of movement and stillness, of steadiness and ease. Our centres offer a variety of yang yoga (primarily Vinyasa and Hatha-based) and yin yoga. We offer meditation because we feel all physical yoga should lead to stillness and the ability to sit with ourselves and find peace within. We also take students on deeper dives with workshops, immersions and retreats, which give them a wonderful opportunity to submerge themselves in the teachings while building a strong community with meaningful connections.

We offer these expressions of yoga to reflect both the dynamic and the still within us and within life – to allow our practice to both strengthen and lengthen, to warm and to cool, to find balance within the dance of the heat of the sun and the cooling light of the moon, to harmonise the energies of the masculine and the feminine within us, to offer our students a chance to stoke the internal fire through movement and Vinyasa yoga, and to cool the inner environment with Yin yoga and meditation, to bring equity. Finally, we allow the practice to be led by the seasons, nourishing our inner body with seasonally appropriate practices.

    The beginning of spring, for example, is a time to sweat, to move with the upwelling of energy as the world creeps out from the slumber of winter – the body has a natural energy we can play with. In the dark of winter, however, we want to conserve our water and energy so we don't want to sweat profusely, and we want the practice to be more nourishing. We'll explore these seasonal themes more on the following pages.

Yang yoga

Vinyasa looks at linking postures with breath, creating a rhythm of movement. So much in nature rocks and undulates. Think of seaweed under the surface of the ocean or river pebbles below the current of a stream, the blades of grass in the kiss of the wind or the resilience of branches in a storm. For us, to move the body in undulating and flowing patterns matched with breathing and awareness is nothing short of magic. There has to, of course, be a balance between stability and fluidity, but the gift of movement is transformative.

Yin yoga

Yin yoga consists of long, slow holds that influence the connective tissues of the body and increase flexibility. We don't use the muscles so much as rest into our ligaments and joints, draping ourselves so we engage the connective tissues and energetic systems of the body. While it's a wonderful practice for flexibility, it also increases our energy, or chi flow, primarily through creating pressure and compression around the meridians and organs.

Our practice

Our offerings at Egg draw from various traditions, with the goal of finding more freedom in our movement and more stillness within: it's akin to placing maps from different traditions one over the other and realising that all roads lead to one. Whether drawn from the Indian or Chinese traditions of yoga or Zen or mindfulness meditation, the heart of yoga is what we aim to share. Similarly with nutrition or other life practices, we blend modern nutrition and science with traditional wisdom, with a focus on extracting the best outcomes, whether they be around the pleasure derived from food, the positive psychological developments or simply greater peace.

Everything we offer at Egg is an extension of what we practise at home, what feels best for us.

The power of wholefoods

If yoga is one pillar of Egg of the Universe, the other is wholefoods. Put simply, our philosophy on wholefoods is about two things: nutrient density and bio-availability. For us that means choosing ingredients that are grown, produced and processed in ways that maintain the highest level of nutrients, then preparing them in ways that unlock their potential, as well as listening to our bodies and addressing their specific needs at different times of year.

If our food is nutrient-dense and rich in elements that our bodies need, then we are far more likely to function better, physically and mentally. It's when we are lacking in nutrients – and this can happen slowly over time – that our bodies can become compromised. One part of a wholefoods philosophy is about seeking ingredients that are produced in ways that maintain their integrity, and the other is what you do in your own kitchen. A wholefoods diet both informs our choices about how to make our food rich in sustenance and also ensures it is easy to assimilate into the body.

Our hope is that through reading this book, you'll be encouraged to support producers and suppliers that promote sustainability and the nurturing of the land. But even more importantly, we hope you gain a better sense of what good food is, and how to go about cooking it for yourself on a daily basis. In this way, you'll become part of a cultural shift based around a more flavourful and nutritious form of eating that contributes to an overall sense of wellbeing.

There are, of course, basic guidelines, principles and food philosophies you can follow, but ultimately everyone's nutritional needs change on a day-to-day basis and the best-placed person to define what they are is you! The way to explore this more fully is through taking note of your experiences as you eat, tuning into the emotional and physical senses of the body and learning to recognise your body and mind as one entity; this is also another form of yoga. Our approach is about bringing these mindful practices to bear on how we eat throughout the seasons.

HOW I DISCOVERED WHOLEFOODS

The love of food, and the knowledge of how to make it, is for most an inherited skill and a passion that evolves through generations.

I was very lucky that my maternal grandmother was a great traditional English cook, and my mother was amazing, too. For those fortunate enough to be brought up where good food is central to the family traditions, this lays the foundation for both a healthy relationship with food and a good diet.

In my late 20s, I developed a digestive issue; it wasn't a serious illness but for me it had a big impact. I just didn't feel good, and having been pretty fit and healthy all my life this didn't seem right. Not being able to get clear answers from my doctor, I began exploring holistic approaches to diet and digestion, though none of them really resonated with me in terms of striking a balance between nutrition and deliciousness. There were all the trendy diets – paleo, low-fat, low-carb, and so on – but nothing seemed to add up to a cohesive approach.

It was only when I explored the wholefoods movement that I finally found a concept that had withstood the test of time, with its underlying theory being relevant to every culture around the world. It seemed to be woven through with common sense that was perfectly aligned to what my instincts had always told me – how could beautifully creamy butter be bad when I could feel how good it was in my bones? This philosophy wholeheartedly supports a vision of living in harmony with the land while feasting on the goodness of its produce. It also encompasses a universal principle of eating and food production that, for me, holds the answer to many of the key environmental, nutritional and cultural issues of our time.

In the Western world there's a deep disconnection from the land and the means of production, and with it an absence of basic knowledge around food. This ignorance is fertile ground for endless dietary fads and trends to emerge. With the wholefoods movement, I discovered that good food didn't need to be about denial. Food was the champion that could take a central role in health. There was no need to deny yourself in order to eat well – as long as you ate a balanced wholefoods diet and followed some basic principles, then you could actually have your proverbial cake and eat it too.

The yoga of eating

Yoga isn't just something we practise on a mat – it can be extended to life in general, and of course to our experience of eating, whether we are vegan, vegetarian, flexitarian or omnivorous. What many practitioners of yoga discover, especially those who continue long-term, is that its true magic is not found in the physical by-products of better strength, flexibility and mental clarity, but in the blossoming of a greater sense of connectivity. The core activity in yoga can be seen as learning to connect more deeply with our body and our emotions, while becoming aware of our minds. This then naturally opens up our ability to refine and develop our relationship with food.

The practice of the yoga of eating is simple. Here is a guide to get you started; if you apply these steps every now and then to an eating experience, you'll notice the gifts that they bring.

Step 1: Bringing awareness to the table

The triggers for consumption are many, but they generally fall into two different categories:

1. **Physical need**
    The body needs sustenance to survive, and our bodies are incredibly well tuned to let us know firstly when there is a physical need, and secondly what it is that's required to meet it. These signals can become confused by the availability of an abundance of poor-quality foods coupled with a mindless approach to what we're eating. To refine your own instincts, listen and respond to the cues from your body. Are you thirsty? What do you need to eat? What path feels best when addressing these desires? If you hone these senses and marry them with sound nutritional guidance you'll begin to refine and re-attune your physical instincts and desires.

2. **Emotional need**
    Often with food and drink we become attuned to putting emotional needs before physical ones. Running our business is sometimes a desperately challenging experience (yes, the irony of being stressed about running a yoga and wellness business isn't lost on us!), and yes, we'll sometimes soothe the pain with too much coffee or food or booze. Even though there may sometimes be an underlying physical craving for these substances, once you're habituated to them, your body typically asks for more. The key is to recognise the choices we make, and understand them: this balances the equation, and allows us to make better choices next time. Our philosophy is to explore whether we're reaching for these foods out of habit, or whether there's a true underlying physical requirement.

In both of the above cases, the yoga of eating encourages us to notice what desires materialise, then gently delve into the roots of where they've come from. We try to avoid bringing in any story around them that may lead to judgements of whether this desire or choice of foods is either good or bad. Developing understanding, awareness and mindfulness around eating is the goal.

Step 2: Let's eat

Once we've brought awareness to what we desire to eat and what may have triggered that desire, we then proceed to the best part. We eat what we desire without judgement, the only core goal being that we are charged with extracting the greatest amount of pleasure as possible from the act of eating. The way we do this is to allow ourselves the time and space to fully explore our food. When eating mindfully, the aim is to pause and bring attention back to the act of eating itself, regardless of how busy our day is.

There are some basic steps you can take when approaching this. First, when you are sitting down to eat, give yourself time to relax before getting started: take a moment to be aware of your body, allow a couple of deep breathing cycles to pass through your system, consciously relax your belly. This pause before you eat is an essential step on the road to a deeper and more meaningful relationship with your diet, and it also aids digestion.

Step 3: Listen to your body

With each bite, as the flavours and textures in your mouth begin to subside, turn your attention to how you feel. Was the experience of eating more mindfully interesting or not? Did it make you feel impatient? Do you feel satisfied by the food you just ate or do you want more? Explore these questions and follow your instincts towards more or less, or even different foods. Keep this up until you're finished eating, then extend this awareness out beyond the meal to track how you feel in the minutes and hours afterwards. On a higher plane, the question is whether the food you just ate has left you feeling satisfied and well nourished, or whether you feel an underlying sense of anxiousness that could be attributed to not having eaten well.

This practice of listening deeply to your body, mind and emotions and how they relate to your food will become more refined over time, evolving into a knowledge of what nourishes and serves you and what doesn't, such that it becomes more second nature than an active pursuit.

Elements and energies

A few years ago we became more interested in listening to the way our bodies felt during different times of the year. We would notice, for example, the urge in the early parts of spring to sort out long-forgotten cupboards or corners of our home. A rising energy of getting stuff done. It wasn't a cerebral decision but rather an upwelling of energy from within – we suddenly found ourselves digging around and cleaning out old books we no longer needed or clothes we no longer wore. As we descended into the winter months, we would notice a slight feeling of sadness and a real need to nest a little more and do a little less. We began to notice that during autumn our allergies might worsen or we might feel more of a tightness in our lungs.

This is, of course, all supported by the principles of Five Element Theory and traditional Chinese medicine. But it wasn't until we felt it in our bodies that these theories came to life. Over time, we've come to trust these theories as pillars and to lean into them at pivotal points of the year. We use them to pause and listen to the call of our deeper selves and come back to our centre. The natural world around us can provide us with the cues we need to realign and refocus.

This, then, guides the structure in each chapter of this book. We acknowledge which organs and elements are important in each season, and take inspiration from nature to guide our practice. For us, staying connected to the subtle shifts of the seasons helps us feel more present in the ordinary moments of the day, and allows us to find joy among the details, like the first daffodil of spring or the scent of flowers in the full bloom of summer.

With these chapters as a guide, you can begin to embrace the invitation of each season and adjust your own habits and routines to live in a more connected way, guided by movement, breath and stillness.

What are wholefoods?

The way we connect with our food is based on our own senses and nutritional compass, but at Egg of the Universe, we choose to couple this with a wholefoods philosophy. To integrate mindful eating with the opportunity to nourish our bodies. Just as meditation can deepen the experience of yoga and expand your awareness, an understanding of wholefoods can deepen your experience of mindful eating, by offering up foods with higher nutritional integrity and teaching you to get the most out of them for your body.

If we're lucky, from an early age we've been instilled with a notion of what 'wholesome' foods are – say, brown bread over white – and that they're better for us because they contain more nutrients. For many of us, this is about as far as the idea of eating wholefoods goes. Maybe it includes eating more vegetables, or eating organic, or eating poorly cooked brown rice while failing to pretend you're happy about it!

A wholefoods philosophy is about choosing foods that are as close to their natural state as possible. It's also about going beyond what's on the plate to look at how our food is farmed, grown or gathered, if and how it's processed and what additives are used, how it comes to us (via the supermarket, farmers' markets or other sources) and then how we prepare it. It recognises that many traditional practices, be they on the farm or in our kitchen, are based on getting the most nutritional value out of our food. These practices aren't romantic or abstract, they're part of our cultural heritage – things that our grandparents were doing, and their grandparents, going back generations. These techniques inform how we could best prepare and choose our food, whether by soaking, sprouting and fermenting our grains, by choosing particular cuts of meat from animals raised a certain way, or in how we preserve or cook our fruits, vegetables and dairy. And, of course, they also encourage us to eat seasonally.

These cultural traditions also give us a pretty clear narrative on what the best fats are to use and what sugars and other carbohydrates are sensible. All these traditional food preparation techniques would have developed over many generations – hundreds, if not thousands, of years prior to modern science. They would have been refined by balancing the practicality of needing to feed people as efficiently as possible against the collective sense of what was most nourishing for the group.

At its best, a wholefoods diet is about eating food that tastes amazing, but that also takes you on a journey into yourself, your local community, and the wider global community beyond. There's a lot more to it than just choosing brown bread over white, but it's also pretty simple once you wrap your head around it. By applying some basic knowledge and simple techniques, you can easily dive into a wholefoods diet.

The wholefoods pantry

All good cooking comes down to the quality of your ingredients. In a wholefoods kitchen, this is no less vital. With a little cooking knowledge, you can easily create foods that taste good, but in order to satisfy deeper aspects of our nourishment, food also needs to be full of the nutrients we need to survive and regulate our bodies. This is where you can begin to make profound changes in your kitchen. Every ingredient counts. Your choice of salts, sugars, fats, flours and grains, along with where you source your fresh produce, collectively makes a big difference. These are the key ingredients that fill the cupboards and fridges of kitchens around the world, and they're the source from which our inspiration springs and the magic happens.

They're also one of the primary places where we are already losing the battle. Take a pantry staple such as refined table salt. On its own it probably doesn't make a big difference, but if you are consuming refined salt as well as refined flours and sugars, overly processed foods and poor fats and oils, your body is missing out on a whole host of minerals and nutrients that have been stripped out. The picture becomes a lot bigger. By thinking about how we choose our staples, and where and how our fruits, vegetables, meat and fish are grown and reared, we start to gain more perspective on how the little things can add up to a whole package.

The fantastic news is that by gradually changing what you have in the kitchen, and by developing your culinary knowledge, you can start to make progress immediately, and your body will feel the results just as fast. Think of it less as an enforced diet, and more as a path of discovery, supported by the 'yoga of eating' philosophy detailed earlier.

Aim to stock your pantry with as many unrefined foods as possible. Take a look at everything you normally buy, and over time you can transition to different choices that better support you. Following are our recommendations for some of the most common items in your pantry.

Salt

Salt is essential, both for our bodies and for creating balance of flavour in our cooking. It has the power to turn a dish from something bland and uninviting into a masterpiece with just a few pinches. Salt has been somewhat demonised in recent times, but there's nothing wrong with it if it's eaten in moderation and in its natural form: there's a reason we crave salt and that our tears and sweat are salty, after all. The issue with salt, we believe, is when it's used excessively in processed foods as a flavour enhancer or preservative. Moving away from processed foods or being discerning about what we're buying can serve to lower our salt intake, which means that the salt we're giving our body (it is a vital nutrient) is in a form we're choosing via our instincts and tastebuds. For us, that means looking for natural sea salts that haven't been bleached or refined any more than absolutely necessary. These salts are plentiful in minerals, and might have some colour, as with Celtic-style sea salt or pink salt, and can sometimes even be slightly damp, while the flaky texture adds interest to dishes, too. We recommend unrefined sea salt for our recipes, but try different types for different mineral contents and flavours.

Fats

On a basic level, the wholefoods movement champions fats that have been traditionally used around the world, while warning against many of the refined vegetable oils that have been introduced over the last few decades. The focus is on what's good in terms of taste and nutrition, as well as what's safe to cook with.

From a wholefoods perspective there's a recognition that fats are super nutrient-dense, and that when we eat them our bodies feel satisfied, thereby reducing our desire to eat excessively. The missteps of the low-fat fad popular with previous generations were that often fats were replaced with a high amount of sugar, under the guise of it being 'healthier'. Supermarkets were flooded with low-fat, high-sugar processed foods. A wholefoods approach recognises that fats are inherently satisfying and make you feel full. To us it made so much sense: why would we instinctively crave crispy chicken skin, enjoy butter so much, love cheese or find avocados so deeply satisfying if they weren't okay for us to eat? If you take a mindful approach to eating, and embrace eating 'good' fats, you'll realise as we did that you get more from eating less when your diet is rich in good fats.

Having an array of fats in your diet is essential for good health. The core question is the quality of the fat and what type of fat you are consuming.

The two fats we like to use the most in cooking are olive oil and coconut oil. As well as tasting great in the right dish, coconut oil has anti-microbial and anti-fungal properties. We do, however, tend to cook more with olive oil, although we avoid using it at high temperatures because it can denature; the very best olive oils we keep simply for salads and for finishing dishes.

We avoid cheap vegetable oils such as corn, soy, canola and sunflower oils. Almost invariably these oils denature when cooked and have a high omega-6 content, which can throw your body out of balance, while offering very little in the way of flavour or nutrition. Peanut and sesame oils can be more readily used for cooking, but have the same omega-6 issue. Look for cold-pressed versions and try to blend or mix them with other oils with higher omega-3 levels to balance them out. Some other interesting oils with good flavour include macadamia, walnut, flaxseed, avocado and pumpkin-seed oils. If you build up a collection of these, and store them well, you can use them to make exceptional dressings for seasonal leaves and salads.

If you aren't vegetarian or vegan, then your choice of fats to cook with expands into even more interesting areas. Butter is back in, duck fat can rock your world, pork fat is incredibly delicious and beef fat does amazing things for your tummy. All of these are brilliant for cooking as they have high smoke points and don't denature at high heat. Further, if you can source them from animals that are raised well with room to roam free and access to pasture, then your body will be all the better for it.

Every ingredient counts. Your choice of salts, sugars, fats, flours and grains, along with where you source your fresh produce, collectively makes a big difference.

Grains, seeds, legumes and flours

Our priority here is to source grains, seeds, legumes and flours in their most 'whole' form, so that the base still retains some vitality. In many cases, imported grains, or those processed on an industrial scale, are irradiated or sprayed and can take a long time to make it to our plates. Buying local and organic seeds and grains wherever possible circumvents this issue and often results in eating products with a higher nutritional value.

We take a common-sense approach. You don't need to forgo white breads and rice completely, but where you can incorporate more wholegrains, try to. For us, it also means understanding the pleasures in preparing and eating these foods. Brown rice can be delicious if it's cooked and seasoned properly, but if it's not it's no more appealing than roughage (and understandably this sends people back to the quick-cook white-rice queue!).

The trend with flours has been to refine them to within an inch of their life, then – as if that wasn't bad enough – to bleach them to make them white. More natural versions of refined white flour are readily available if you look for them – they might have a hint of grey or brown in them, but this is how they're meant to look! Refined flours are often fortified with the nutrients that were stripped out in the first place, and in forms less easily digested by the body. It's also important to remember that as industrialisation has progressed, the variety in the strains of wheat available has dropped significantly. As much as we're for progress and development, we're also interested in retaining genetic diversity and having a spectrum of flours and grains available. This, in the long run, translates to more interesting and better flavours, and – crucially – better nutritional outcomes on the plate.

Our main advice is to start incorporating more wholegrains into your diet by looking at some of the different ones out there. If you don't love brown rice, consider a semi-refined version instead, or try a brown basmati rice or even wild black rice. If you can tolerate gluten, explore options such as spelt or freekeh. Look at barley or buckwheat, try using lentils in salads and investigate the vast array of dried legumes. There are all kinds of grains, seeds and legumes that have great nutritional value as well as interesting textures and flavours; you just need to know how to prepare them well. Soaking is one of these ways; see page 39 for more on that.

Sugar

Until relatively recently, apart from being able to gorge on ripe seasonal fruits or feast on wild honey, sugar wasn't a large part of our diet. The majority of our carbohydrate intake would have come from other food sources, which generally would have introduced sugars into our bloodstream more slowly. Sugar now, in comparison, is readily available and incredibly cheap, which means that we see it in almost everything.

But this isn't just about quantity. From a wholefoods perspective, beyond acknowledging that too much sugar really isn't good for us, it's also about the quality and flavour of the sugar. A wholefoods approach seeks out sweetness in its most natural form. Unrefined sugars, such as raw honey, maple syrup or rapadura (dehydrated cane juice), have much greater flavour than fully refined white sugar. Many unrefined sugars contain valuable B vitamins to go with minerals such as magnesium and chromium, which in themselves play a role in supporting blood-sugar regulation; these are typically stripped out in more refined sugars.

Our approach to sugar is to choose less refined versions, and to unlock the natural sweetness in many of the other ingredients we eat on a daily basis. We also try to marry sweet foods with good fats and proteins so we're not giving our body a pure sugar rush all at once. This way, our sweeter dishes generally contain less sugar than conventional versions, while having more flavour and greater nutrient density, which then means that smaller amounts satisfy you more.

A mindful approach to vegetables

Do you ever marvel at the shape and form of vegetables? We should all take the time to ponder the beauty of the bounty that comes from the earth. Cut a purple cabbage in half and admire the pattern, leave your pumpkins sitting proudly on the counter for a week or so, or lose yourself in the repeating patterns of broccoli or one of the coolest vegetables on the planet – the cauliflower. We are so lucky to be living in a place and time where such an abundant variety of vegetables and herbs are available, especially if you step outside the supermarket into farmers' markets, or even grow your own.

Fruits and vegetables

Seasonality is key to our approach to fruit and veg. For many of us, an urban lifestyle has meant our connection to the natural cycle of the seasons has been partially severed. Due to globalisation, we also have greater access to fruits all year round, which wouldn't previously have been available to us.

Traditionally, many cultures around the world lived in a dance with nature and understood deeply that we are a product of the environment; a reality to be deeply respected in order to thrive and survive. It's no coincidence that our nutritional needs are often directly linked to what is seasonally available to us locally. We encourage you to dive more deeply into what's available locally and seasonally throughout the year. This is how you can begin to reconnect to your natural surroundings and to foods that are the most nurturing for the season you are in. By basing your diet on local and seasonal produce, you are more likely to be eating the foods your body needs most, and you're also more likely to be supporting local farmers as well as reducing the environmental impact of your food choices. We love to shop at our local farmers' markets as much as possible. This inspires us to eat seasonally, but also it's an energising and inspirational place for any cook, and comes with the added bonus of produce free from packaging or plastics.

Our recipes feature many different methods of cooking vegetables for a delicious result, be it boiling, steaming, frying or roasting, along with advice on how to season properly. Our hope is that you'll learn to create great dishes from the simplest of vegetables, which may even relegate meat and fish to the sidelines.

The reality is that if you cook your vegetables appropriately and season judiciously according to your body's wants and desires, then a simple dish of steamed greens can become the champion. A tray of mixed roast vegetables with salad and good sauces becomes a feast – not to mention how good roast spuds (just like my grandmother made) can be, or how a simple steamed turnip or cabbage with parsley, lemon and olive oil can transform your impressions of it from an otherwise boring or simple food into one that you can savour. We're very much in favour of people discovering the fun and excitement of a more vegetarian style of cooking.

Meat and fish

A discussion around the consumption of meat and fish within a yoga and wholefoods book might be a controversial one for some. The key thrust of our approach is to encourage you to connect with your instincts (no surprise here by now, we hope). If they lead you down the path of less and eventually no animal products, then great, but if you are instinctively led down another path, then nutritionally this is probably more sensible for your body – for us, this is yoga!

We seek to source all our animal products from animals that have either been wild-caught or raised in accordance with their nature – for many this means being allowed to roam free over pasture, which is mostly supported by organic and permaculture farming methods. Animals that have been raised this way tend to have far better flavour and a higher nutritional profile, not to mention a much more humane existence.

We also subscribe to the no-waste nose-to-tail approach of consuming meat, which is consistent with the way our forebears would have cooked. Nutritionally, many organ meats are rich in the fat-soluble vitamins A, D, E and K, as well as omega-3 fatty acids, which are all hugely important for robust human health. If you go into most supermarkets or many butchers, however, you tend only to get the choice cuts, often denuded of their natural fats and sadly too often sourced from industrial farms. This is a waste, both morally and nutritionally, and it's one of the things that needs to change if we are going to continue eating animals in a sustainable and healthy way. In many traditional preparations meat and fish are eaten in all forms: raw, rare, slow-cooked and often fermented (think of salami, for example). Then the bones are used to create nutrient-dense broths.

The consumption of fish is a tricky issue in our current times. A diet rich in seafood has consistently been shown to be one of the healthiest in the world, with seafood one of the highest sources of animal proteins and fats on the planet. We are, however, faced with collapsing stocks due to overfishing and pollution. So as much as we love fish – we get very excited about raw fish, fish roe and shellfish, and love eating seafood every which way – we try to choose sustainably sourced seafood and vote with our wallets to protect our oceans. If that also means reducing our consumption and making seafood more of a special-occasion thing, then so be it. Then there's the issue of heavy metals in larger fish – those at the top of the food chain. Our best advice is to find sources you trust, and keep sustainability in mind as much as possible.

We use the following guiding principles when it comes to the consumption of meat and fish:

- Try to only consume meats and fish that have been wild-caught or farmed according to sound principles. This may mean buying more expensive produce, but quality over quantity is the go.

- Eat nose-to-tail and explore different cuts and methods – rare, raw, slow-cooked, fermented.

- Get into making bone broths – this will change your world.

- Eat instinctively: if you really want steak, there's probably a good reason. If meat really isn't doing it for you, then try going without.

Dairy

It's mostly only in the West that we have milk in its uncultured form. Before industrialisation, Europeans consumed milk as yoghurt, cheeses or curds and whey. When dairy was consumed uncultured it would certainly have been unpasteurised as this process only came in with the advent of the industrial revolution. Milk at its most natural – straight from the cow – is an amazing food. It's full of its own beneficial bacteria, which are great for our digestion, plus a whole raft of other nutritional goodies such as amino acids, vitamins, minerals and good fats. The modern processes of pasteurisation and homogenisation destroy, neutralise or denature many of those benefits.

Pasteurisation particularly is a controversial subject, so much so that raw milk in Australia is only available as a cosmetic product. The heating process changes the makeup of milk, meaning that some of the benefits become less pronounced. We believe that, with advances in testing methods and cold-chain technology, raw milk is something we should be able to safely and confidently consume. Leaving aside the health benefits, raw milk just tastes completely delicious – like it's alive with goodness. And since the lactic acids aren't destroyed in the pasteurisation process, if it's left long enough, it'll split out naturally into curds and whey. The curds can be used almost like a cottage cheese, spread onto toast or whisked through a savoury pancake batter. The whey, meanwhile, not only makes a nutritious drink, but can be added to smoothies to boost the protein levels, or be used as a lively starter for activating seeds or pickling fruits and vegetables.

The practice of fermenting or souring milk is found in almost all traditional groups that keep or kept herds. This process breaks down lactose and casein, thus partially digesting it and increasing the probiotic nature of the milk and its bioavailability. Culturing produces numerous enzymes that help the body absorb calcium and other minerals. Beyond this are all the traditional forms of making amazing cheeses, which find so many different and unique forms around the world.

Those with dairy sensitivity are more likely to be able to eat fermented dairy products since much of the lactose has been turned into lactic acid, while the presence of lactase aids further digestion in the body. Raw or not, there are also ways of fermenting dairy that can really help people recovering from dairy intolerances. Harry brought his own digestive system back into balance with a number of probiotic foods, but milk kefir and coconut kefir are two of our favourites. We run through the method for making your own kefir on page 255.

Unlocking nutrients in wholefoods

There's often a misconception that a wholefoods diet is largely about eating more brown rice and piously having a handful of nuts when you're peckish. The truth is the concept extends wider and deeper into every area of food, with different techniques to master and concepts to grasp within every area. The best part is that none of it is too hard. Soaking, sprouting and fermenting are some of the simplest ways to bring a wholefoods philosophy into your life. All of these are processes designed to help unlock the hidden nutrients in our food. Soaking and sprouting in particular apply to nuts, grains, seeds and legumes, while fermentation can be used in a number of different applications. In some cases the adjustments are subtle, but we hope that these simple changes will have a profound effect on your eating.

As with many forgotten techniques, soaking, sprouting and fermenting were common in pre-industrial societies across the globe. Preservation is one factor, but typically these processes improve nutritional value, as well as unlocking nutrients for the body to access.

Soaking

With the benefits of modern science, we know that a majority of grains and seeds contain phytic acid and/or digestive enzyme inhibitors that can impede the absorption of vital nutrients and minerals. Simply soaking grains and seeds in water with a little salt or acid allows enzymes, lactobacilli and other helpful micro-organisms to break down and neutralise the phytic acid and other digestive inhibitors. The added kick is that soaking unlocks beneficial enzymes for digestion and also increases the vitamin content.

Soaking is a classic example of how a simple wholefoods process increases the nutritional value of foods we eat every day, while also aiding digestion. Since soaking is the first step in kickstarting germination, it's important that you're starting with ingredients that come from a good source and still have some vitality.

Soaking makes sense if we think about it: typically a nut or seed would need to make it out the other side of an animal's digestive system and still germinate; the phytic acid makes it harder to digest, meaning it comes out ready to sprout and grow. Soaking unlocks those nutrients, transferring them from the plant to us. It's why when we eat too many nuts we might feel a little sick or lethargic. Nuts that are activated (soaked then dehydrated), on the other hand, are more easily digestible, and they taste better, too. Typically these cost a bomb in a shop, but doing it yourself is simple – just soak them overnight in plenty of salted water, drain, then dry them in a low oven for 12–24 hours.

Soaking and activation is good for other foods too. Try soaking your porridge oats overnight with a squeeze of lemon juice or some yoghurt, for example. The process both activates them and also makes them faster to cook (who needs quick oats anyway!). What you'll find when you begin activating your oats is that they'll keep you energised for longer and leave you feeling even more satisfied. If you know you're having pancakes for breakfast, try soaking the flour the night before. One of the reasons that sourdough is so feted is the long, slow process of fermentation and hydration – ie soaking – that helps the flour break down. This is particularly the case for wheat breads where a more traditional approach and long proving process with a natural bread starter helps to make the gluten more digestible.

Sprouting

Sprouting works in much the same way as soaking, but it means allowing the nut, grain or seed to sprout into a young plant. The process of germination produces vitamin C but also changes the composition of the nut, grain or seed, increasing the vitamin B content and producing numerous enzymes that aid digestion. Complex sugars, which can contribute to intestinal gas, are broken down during sprouting, and a portion of the starch is transformed into sugar. Sprouting also deactivates aflatoxins, which are potent carcinogens found in grains.

These mini sprouts are full of so much goodness – we eat them whenever we can – and it's so easy to do on your kitchen counter. Once they've sprouted, the little lovelies can either be thrown into salads, sprinkled over dishes, or cooked with – we use a lot of sprouted buckwheat in the café simply because it's so good and there is just something about it that makes your body say yes!

Fermenting, preserving and pickling

These techniques have been knocking about in many forms since the beginning of recorded time, to preserve the abundant excess of a crop in summer or autumn to make it available through the winter months. These processes essentially harness the power of naturally occurring bacteria which, when provided with the right environment and a beneficial food source, can kickstart the fermentation process and create a change in the base food. Over time, fermentation has become understood as highly beneficial and is revered in many cultures as an essential part of their identity.

In many ways, the modern mind has been inoculated with the idea that bacteria is bad, and that we should live in a sterilised world where none of these things can touch us. The reality, however, is that we're surrounded by bacteria all the time, and carry in our bodies more bacteria than the cells that make us up. Beneficial bacteria is all around us: on our skin, in our eyes, ears, mouths and everywhere else. In our digestive system, in particular, we carry around one to two kilograms of bacteria, which are incredibly important for our overall health and wellbeing. Simply put, without them we wouldn't be alive: mess with the balance of these bacteria and pay the consequences.

In past times, we would have consumed some form of fermented probiotic food with nearly every meal and so our gut would have maintained a happy equilibrium. But in our race to make our food safe for the masses (which is important – salmonella poisoning isn't fun), we have inadvertently discarded many of these techniques.

Fast forward to today and the traditional method of lacto-fermenting vegetables and fruits is finally re-entering the mainstream. Thanks in part to the wholefoods movement, and the work of people such as Sally Fallon (the modern mother of wholefoods) and Sandor Katz (the godfather of fermentation), this type of preservation method has been saved from the scrapheap.

If you pop to the local supermarket and buy some sauerkraut, you'll most likely end up with a jar of boiled shredded cabbage that has been preserved in sugar and vinegar. While it may have a nice sweet-sour tang, it's a far cry from the beauty of the real thing that's been packed in salt and naturally fermented. Go back only a few generations in Germany and sauerkraut would have been made in autumn with the excess harvest, which would have been shredded, salted and then trodden into barrels to get the juices flowing, before being sealed and buried underground until the following spring. The naturally occurring lactobacilli would then be given the chance to go to work, consuming the starchy sugars of the cabbage. Acid and gas are produced as byproducts, and it's this acid and the expanding microbe population that both protects the pickle from other, potentially harmful, microbes, and preserves the vegetable. The resulting kraut is a live pickle that will be full of great acidity and enzymes to aid digestion, as well as being highly probiotic and vitamin-rich. When paired with a fatty sausage, say, these elements will then help the body digest fats and proteins. Again, improved nutritional value, and better digestion. There are plenty of ferments and pickle recipes in this book for you to try, both simple and more involved.

Today the traditional method of lacto-fermenting vegetables and fruits is finally starting to re-enter the mainstream.

MANY MOMENTS
OFTEN

Meditation was always something I knew I should do but it remained on my New Year's resolutions lists for many years before it became a genuine daily practice. Years later, what was initially born from motivation to reduce stress or disconnect for just a few moments, slowly became a habit. I now see it as a central pillar in my life, a way for me to feel grounded and present as life unfolds and something that gives me a heightened sense of tenderness towards both myself and the world around me.

After practising meditation for a while, it begins to reach into the very corners of your day, bringing added awareness to even the smallest acts. You may find yourself waiting for the kettle to boil and using it as a chance to feel your feet on the floor, relax into your lower belly and take a few deep breaths. You may use the minutes spent waiting at the bus stop to feel the sun on your back and to listen to the hubbub of activity around you. It might be as simple as paying added attention to a hug you have with a friend or a goodnight kiss with your children.

As we begin to cultivate this attention, in many moments and often throughout the day, it allows us to step from one conscious moment to another. These moments of awareness can then often make up the most poignant parts of our day, creating a bridge between disconnection and chaos to a more grounded way of feeling our way through each day.

Being able to connect meaningfully to these little moments brings greater happiness and takes the pressure off the big moments – waiting for the job promotion or the new car or the holidays. Instead you can extract joy from the ordinary and find the profundity in the little things – memories, feelings, laughter, love, growth, insight and understanding. That lovely saying by Jon Kabat-Zinn describes this notion: 'The little things? The little moments? They aren't little.'

I practise meditation to help manage myself in life. To feel steadier while parenting our two kids, maintaining my key relationships, running our business and taking care of the myriad tasks and daily responsibilities

Moments of awareness can often make up the most poignant parts of our day, creating a bridge between disconnection and chaos to a more grounded way of feeling. It's being able to connect meaningfully to these little moments that brings about greater happiness and takes the pressure off the big moments. The most beautiful things in life are not things but memories, feelings, laughter, love, growth, insight and understanding.

that go with it all. I use my practice to feel less discombobulated and fractured, with the intention of staying as grounded as possible and learning to remain centred (at least some of the time) in the various terrains of life. There are now many moments throughout the day when I'll bring my full attention to the foreground and notice my body, my breath, the emotions making up the mood of my inner body, my mindscape, the sounds I can hear. Doing this helps me to anchor my attention in the here and now, then proceed with a greater sense of ease.

Meditation has so many different methods and ultimately has to be experienced for yourself to be fully understood. For us, the type of meditation we do may well change over the years as we develop and our capacity to sit along with our awareness gets stronger. There are so many styles and beliefs and ways in, but the method is less important than how you are within your own practice.

Our firmest belief, though, is that all roads lead to the same centre, so don't get too caught up with the method. Keep it light and know that it will change as you do. Most of all, trust that through learning to sit still, and being present in our own company, the rest will happen on its own.

Following the seasons

Spring

element
wood

organs
**liver and gall
bladder**

Characteristics of spring

If we look to the natural world, in spring we can draw inspiration from what we observe and feel happening around us. After the sleep of winter, we see new grass growing and, in some parts of the world, pushing through snow towards the sun. We can see fresh, tiny, bright green buds on the ends of bare, wintry branches, new leaves budding from trees, an explosion of flowers, the energy of the earth rousing from the slumber of winter. If we have taken the time to rest during the colder, more inward-focused months, we may feel a new up-welling of energy within us. Almost like taking a huge deep breath, spring is the start of a new cycle and of new life. Nature changes around us, bursting forth with vitality, and we can often feel this intrinsically within ourselves.

For us, spring is the time to let go of the more internal and sluggish states of winter, both physically and emotionally, making room for fresh growth and inspiration. During this season especially it's important to be mindful of what your body craves and desires. This is a time when we naturally tend to eat less, or even fast, and cleanse the body after the heavier and often more fatty foods of winter. In looking towards Eastern cultures, this season is focused on supporting and clearing the 'wood element' and the organs of the liver and gall bladder – we find the best way to do this is to undergo a period of simple eating or cleansing.

Our approach with food at Egg is to combine the traditional wisdom of the wholefoods philosophy with influence from ancient healing methodologies, while always staying mindful of modern scientific research and understanding. Our advice will always be that you need to connect via your senses to that which truly nourishes you, but if you have any specific goals you wish to achieve through the season – be they weight loss or cleansing – seek advice from a health practitioner of your choosing.

optimism

desire
for change

Spring

adaptability

hopefulness

Emotions of spring

We may find ourselves cleaning out cupboards, starting new projects at home or at work, sorting out old clothes, dusting the shelves and so on. This natural energy to start fresh, shed a skin in a way, is an intuitive response to the energy of the season. It's also a time when we can feel a restlessness, an irritation or anxiety as our inner energy grows.

We've found this inner restlessness can often be remedied through taking direct action, with spring presenting a great opportunity to clean the physical body with a simple cleanse or adjustment of the way we eat. All through winter, we tend to eat more warming foods – dominated by braises, soups and broths – and tolerate very little raw and cold food, whereas in spring we crave more raw foods, salads, juices and smoothies, and in smaller quantities. After the inward-looking nature of winter, we find ourselves wanting to step out of our warm coats and amp up the exercise a bit. It's a great time of year to sweat and to move the body. To feel strong and fit. Spring is naturally the time of year to work hard at realising the projects you want to create so that in summer, you will be able to 'harvest' the rewards.

Foods of the season

Our diet through this season should be among the lightest of the year, including pungent and sweet flavours, which support and reflect the upward energy that surrounds us.

Fresh young vegetables such as carrots and beetroot, along with fresh greens, sprouts and sprouted seeds and grains, provide beautiful yet light nourishment. You can include lots of raw and lightly cooked foods, while limiting heavy, salty and fatty foods. To support the liver and gall bladder it's best to eat moderately, avoiding late meals. Strong foods and spices, such as members of the onion family, mustard greens, turmeric, horseradish and rosemary, are effective at stimulating the liver, while sweet foods, such as baby carrots, beets and grains, along with natural sugars, can harmonise with the natural yang energy of spring. Bitter and sour foods, such as apple cider vinegar, lemon and grapefruit, radish, quinoa, dandelion and chamomile, are all excellent for reducing liver excess. Chlorophyll-rich leafy greens are ideal to help with detoxification.

The general call of the organs for this season is to detoxify and refresh, so it's a great season to rest the liver and gall bladder and nourish and renew their vibrancy. We've included some simple and safe ways of doing this. Overall, the liver likes less food, less sugar and less alcohol, so it is a great season to have some time off some of these.

To do in spring:
- Begin your day early with a brisk walk or yang practice.
- Begin new things – at home, in your work, and within yourself.
- Manifest new ideas, move forward, make plans.
- Be assertive, make decisions, be discerning.
- Have vision and hope for the future.

Seasonal practice

Beginning the day with some movement and some awareness creates a still point within us before the day unfolds and our attention is taken elsewhere. The movements of the sun salute have been done over and over for many, many years by many people before us, and are an effective way of moving the spine and transforming our physical and emotional energy. As soon as we start to move with awareness, we can't help but change the way we feel. Try doing each pose separately at first, and then in time, linking them together with breath.

· ·

Surya Namaskar or **Salute to the sun**: A series of postures that help to warm, strengthen and align our entire body.

Cleanse routines

Every culture around the globe traditionally has times of the year that are reserved for mindful or spiritual abstinence. Prior to these cultural traditions developing, early agricultural societies would have had regular periods when many foods weren't available.

. . . .

As hunter-gatherers, we also would have had enforced periods of fasting and deprivation due to our environment; we are naturally attuned to being able to survive for quite a long time without food. The benefits of fasting are that they allow the body to spend its energy on clearing and cleaning the system for longevity and a general sense of wellbeing. It's essential that if you're going to approach a cleanse or fast, it's done mindfully and in full knowledge of what your body actually needs. If you're considering undertaking any fast or cleanse, we recommend seeking advice from a health practitioner of your choosing.

Simple cleanse routine

Simple cleanse – week 1

Visit a holistic doctor, naturopath, traditional Chinese medicine practitioner or otherwise to discuss herbal support for a seasonal cleanse.

Daily focus

- Take time to eat mindfully. Notice what the body is asking for. If you find you're not hungry, skip a meal or eat relatively small amounts. When you do eat, be aware of how you feel afterwards – heavy, bright, happy or anxious.
- Reduce, avoid, or ideally cut out sugar, alcohol and stimulants (including caffeine, but if you are addicted to coffee allow yourself a little green tea to avoid madness!).
- Eat unprocessed high-integrity wholefoods with a local, seasonal focus. Lots of green leafy vegetables and seasonal fruits as desired. Avoid hard-to-digest meats, dairy, gluten and white, starchy foods such as potato and white rice. A little grilled or poached chicken or fish is fine, as are slow-cooked meats and stews.
- At the end of this first week, see how you feel.

Fasting and semi-fasting – week 2

After this initial week of simple living you may like to consider semi or full fasting. Again, full fasting, which involves not consuming anything other than water (plus sometimes coconut water, fruit juice or broth), needs to be undertaken with professional advice and supervision. For us, it's best done on a retreat in nature when you can spend the time just to be and to let go.

Semi-fasting is the best compromise while going about your daily business, and it involves reducing how much you eat to 1–3 meals a day of quite simple foods. When we do this we focus on having very few starchy foods and enjoy lots of green leafy vegetables and good fats, which the body can burn for energy in place of carbohydrates. On a typical semi-fasting day we might consume the following:

- Green smoothie or coconut smoothie (see smoothies, page 258).
- Chicken broth (see page 234).
- Salads and steamed vegetables with good oils, fats and seasonings.
- Slow-cooked meats in broth with small amounts of sprouted lentils or buckwheat.
- Kicharis – kicharis fasting is an ancient Ayurvedic cleansing technique that means you still have plenty of food in your belly; it's a great way to start semi-fasting. Simply eat as much of it as you like, but only eat kicharis for about 3–5 days. For our recipe, see page 159.

Tonics and supplementation

Along with herbal support for your cleanse, you may want to consider taking the following tonics and supplements to encourage the body to cleanse and repair.

- Turmeric-ginger brew in the morning (recipe page 256).
- Aloe vera and chlorophyll, morning and night.
- Probiotics.
- Fish oils and/or flax oil.
- A good multi-vitamin.
- Daily green superfood powder (Shakti's Super Food Blend is great!).

The love cup

One of our original chefs, Brendon Vallejo, came up with this and we remember
the debate around the name. 'Can we call it the love cup? Surely not.' After tasting
it, though, nearly everyone agreed that the name worked – this simple
breakfast cup of love made us all happy.

Serves 2

¼ cup (40 g) chia seeds
200 ml (7 fl oz) coconut water
½ cup (45 g) desiccated coconut
splash of maple syrup
   (optional)
2 mangoes, flesh diced
80 g (2¾ oz) Cashew cream
   (see page 224)
⅔ cup (140 g) mixed berries
80 g (2¾ oz) Activated
   buckwheat granola
   (see page 102)

Soak chia seeds overnight in coconut water to make a chia
pudding (you can get away with much shorter than this but ideally,
soak them for at least an hour). Stir coconut through the pudding
and add a splash of maple syrup and a pinch of salt, if so inclined.

To create the love cup, you just need to layer the ingredients
so they look beautiful. Spoon pudding into serving glasses, then
add the rest of the ingredients in layers starting with the mango,
then cashew cream and berries. Finally, scatter granola on top.

Avo-tomato on toast

This might sound too basic to include in a cookbook, but with simple recipes like this, it's the details that count. This and the Super BLAT (which is basically this recipe, plus bacon) have been the two most popular dishes on our menu since we opened. We like to make the dried tomatoes in large batches that last for a week or two in jars covered in olive oil. We normally leave them quite juicy through the body of the tomato, while allowing the edges to dry out and caramelise.

Serves 2

2 slices sourdough
   spelt bread
1 garlic clove, cut in half
1 large avocado
½ teaspoon apple cider vinegar
   or lemon juice
½ teaspoon olive oil
2 tablespoons tomato relish
   (or Slow-fermented tomato
   chutney, page 226)
Hemp seeds and sumac,
   to serve

OVEN-DRIED TOMATOES
2 kg (4 lb 8 oz) Roma tomatoes
   (or other ripe, in-season
   variety), cut in half
2 tablespoons dried herbs
   (such as thyme, basil
   or oregano)
¼ cup (60 ml) olive oil

For oven-dried tomatoes, preheat oven to 180°C (350°F). Spread tomatoes cut-side up on a roasting tray (they can be close but not on top of each other). Season with salt, sprinkle with dried herbs and drizzle with olive oil. Roast for 15 minutes until softened, but not collapsed, then reduce oven temperature to 90°C and roast slowly for 6–8 hours (or overnight) to dry out.

Toast bread and scrape cut sides of garlic across the surface of each slice of toast. Scoop the avocado flesh from the skin and mash it well, leaving some texture. Season to taste with apple cider vinegar, olive oil and some more salt. Divide avocado evenly between each slice of toast, then top with the tomato relish and two oven-dried tomatoes. Finish with a sprinkle of hemp seeds and sumac.

Green soup

We love cooking this soup in early spring and it's often rolled into action at the end of a weekend when we may have had more wine than is advisable, but want to head into the new week feeling reborn. This is equally enjoyable as a vegetarian dish – just use water as the liquid. If you prefer vegan, omit the butter. Don't be too strict about following this recipe to the letter. This soup is designed to be made with the odds and ends that knock about in the bottom drawer of the fridge. We use everything from parsley stems and the outer layers of leeks to wilted lettuce leaves – they all come together for a fantastic, cleansing flavour.

Serves 4

1-2 tablespoons olive oil or butter (or a mix of both)

1 onion, thinly sliced

2 garlic cloves, crushed

1 leek, roughly chopped

1 celery stalk, roughly chopped

1-2 teaspoons dried herbs (such as thyme, sage or rosemary)

1 thumb-sized piece ginger or fresh turmeric

1-2 carrots, diced

1 root vegetable (such as parsnip or swede), diced

3 large handfuls hardy greens (such as kale or chard), shredded

6 cups (1.5 litres) chicken stock (see page 234)

1 handful green beans, roughly chopped

Juice of 1 lemon (optional)

2 handfuls leafy greens (such as lettuce or bok choy), chopped

2 tablespoons flat-leaf parsley or tarragon, chopped

Preheat a large saucepan over medium–high heat. Add oil or butter along with the onion and a pinch of salt. Stir to begin the sizzle.

Add garlic, then leek and celery, and keep stirring here and there as the vegetables soften and colour in places, about 10 minutes. Add dried herbs (often we'll add a knob of butter here, too), and stir to incorporate.

Continue to layer in the flavours by adding the ginger, carrot and root vegetables. Stir for 5 minutes, then add hardy greens and cook, stirring, for 1–2 minutes until they begin to wilt.

Next, add stock with another pinch or two of salt and a turn of a pepper mill and bring the broth to a simmer. Let this bubble gently away for 20–30 minutes until everything is nice and soft and all the flavours have had the chance to develop.

For the finishing touch, stir in beans; these can retain a little bite. Taste and adjust with extra salt if necessary. To help with the balancing, you can also add a good squeeze of lemon juice at this stage.

As a final flourish, throw in the leafy greens and herbs.

Serve in bowls as is, or try adding a dollop of pesto and a slice of lemon and serve with good toast rubbed with garlic and smeared with butter.

Gluten-free banana bread

We came up with this banana bread after we'd perfected our Paleo bread (see page 155), and it uses the same base with the sprouted buckwheat, which gives it a little more nutrition than your average sweet loaf. We remember testing about five different versions of this on our kids before we got it right – when they finally gave it the thumbs-up, we knew it was ready to be rolled out.

Makes 1 loaf

3 ripe bananas

150 g (5½ oz) Sprouted buckwheat (see page 66)

4 medjool dates, pitted and mashed

1½ cups (150 g) almond meal

150 ml (5 fl oz) maple syrup

4 organic eggs

¼ cup (25 g) arrowroot or tapioca flour

1 teaspoon baking powder

1 teaspoon ground cinnamon

Butter or coconut oil, for greasing and brushing

Preheat oven to 170°C (325°F). Leave one banana aside, then thoroughly mix together all other ingredients, mashing the bananas and dates to a thick batter. Pour into a greased loaf tin, then slice the final banana lengthways and place, cut-side up, on top. Bake for 40 minutes, brush with butter or coconut oil, then bake for a further 5–10 minutes until the top is golden and a skewer withdraws clean.

Yogi miso bowl

This is the kind of brown rice bowl that we find acceptable. If you've seen Harry's TEDx Talk or been to a workshop, you'll know his journey into wholefoods started almost as a reaction to how annoyingly bad most health-food shop brown-rice dishes were back in the naughties. Seasoned and paired with the right ingredients, though, they can be fun – we promise. This is one of those classic vegan dishes to which you can add a poached egg. The addition of the unpasteurised miso and seaweed gives extra nutritional punch, as does the magic of fresh shiitake mushrooms.

Serves 4

· · · · · · · · · · · ·

1⅔ cups (400 g) brown rice (if you can, soak it for 4–8 hours in filtered water, then drain and rinse, otherwise rinse it very well)

2 tablespoons sushi vinegar or rice wine vinegar

1 tablespoon peanut oil

1 teaspoon sesame oil

2 cups (150 g) fresh shiitake or oyster mushrooms

4 tablespoons unpasteurised white miso paste (from health-food shops, and Egg of the Universe)

½ daikon, spiralised to form noodles (or grated)

1 small Lebanese (short) cucumber, shaved into ribbons (with a peeler, mandolin or spiraliser)

2 colourful radishes (red, rainbow or black), thinly sliced on a mandolin

50 g (1¾ oz) dried wakame, soaked in boiling water for 3–5 minutes, then drained

1 tablespoon kimchi (page 239)

2 spring onions (scallions), cut into matchsticks

1 handful coriander (cilantro) leaves

1 teaspoon dried dulse flakes (from health-food shops, and Egg of the Universe)

1 sheet nori, coarsely torn

1 handful snow pea shoots

1 tablespoon toasted white sesame seeds

1 tablespoon toasted black sesame seeds

DRESSING

2 tablespoons olive oil

1 teaspoon sesame oil

1 tablespoon tamari

2 teaspoons mirin

Juice of ½ lime

½ garlic clove, minced

½ teaspoon minced ginger

Cook rice in plenty of salted boiling water for 15–20 minutes – you want to retain some texture but definitely don't undercook it. Drain well, then stir the vinegar through. Cool.

Heat a char-grill pan over high heat to smoking hot. Mix peanut and sesame oils, brush mushrooms with oils, then grill on both sides so they char nicely but maintain their raw quality through the middle, 1–2 minutes each side. Slice into thick bite-sized pieces.

For the dressing, whisk ingredients well and leave to infuse until needed.

Smear bowls with a tablespoonful of miso or place a small serving dish of miso in the base of each bowl. Divide rice among bowls, then add daikon, cucumber and radish. Nestle wakame, kimchi and mushrooms around, then spoon the dressing over the top. Garnish with spring onion, coriander, dulse, nori, shoots and sesame seeds – and prepare to not be bored senseless by brown rice!

Yogi miso bowl, page 62

Sprouted buckwheat salad

Sprouting buckwheat does take a few days, but what you end up with is a super-nutritious sprouted seed that can be seasoned in many different ways. Serve either as the foundation of many dishes, such as our salads or soups, or as an accompaniment to some heartier winter fare, such as our slow-cooked lamb or pork shoulder. It also forms the base of our Paleo bread (see page 155) and our Activated buckwheat granola (see page 102). Seasoned with herbs and kombucha vinaigrette, as it is here, it's a flavourful base that's satisfying and goes with just about anything. If you can't wait for your buckwheat to sprout, you can still activate the seeds by soaking them for 8 hours before cooking.

Makes 1 batch

2½ cups (500 g) raw buckwheat

2-3 handfuls chopped soft green herbs (such as parsley, tarragon, basil and thyme)

Kombucha vinaigrette (see page 227), to taste

Cover buckwheat with filtered water and leave at room temperature for 8 hours (or overnight) to soak.

The next day, strain buckwheat, then run under a cold tap to thoroughly rinse the kernels. It's fully rinsed when the water looks and feels clear, rather than cloudy and sticky.

Tip buckwheat into a bowl, cover, and leave on your kitchen counter overnight. Repeat the rinsing and straining process morning and evening until you see sprouts emerging (a day or so). At this stage you can either keep the buckwheat on the counter until the sprouts are about 2-3 mm long, or keep it in the fridge where it will continue to sprout slowly, cooking it when you like. Otherwise, cook the whole lot and store in the fridge until needed, up to a week.

To cook the sprouted buckwheat, bring a saucepan of salted water to the boil, tip in buckwheat, then bring back to a simmer. Simmer for 3-5 minutes until kernels are tender but still have some texture. Drain and cool. Once cooled, season to taste, stir through herbs and dress with kombucha vinaigrette, adjusting to taste. The buckwheat will soak up a lot of flavour so season liberally.

Classic simple Caesar salad

One of the great salads that's easy to make and to elevate with quality ingredients. This is a dish that is far more than the sum of its parts, and it's perfect for a spring day.

Serves 4
....

2 slices sourdough bread
(or a gluten-free bread
that's worthy of this salad),
cut into croutons
150 ml (5 fl oz) olive oil,
plus extra for drizzling
2 organic eggs
2 garlic cloves
4–6 good anchovies in olive oil
2 teaspoons Worcestershire
sauce (we like ours to be
preservative-free)
1 tablespoon lemon juice
1 cup (100 g) finely grated
good-quality parmesan
1 large cos lettuce, outer leaves
shredded, medium leaves
torn, inner leaves left whole

Preheat oven to 180°C (350°F). Toss bread with a drizzle of olive oil, spread on a baking tray and toast in the oven until golden and crisp, turning halfway, about 5–10 minutes.

Meanwhile, place eggs in a small saucepan of water over medium–high heat and bring to a simmer. Simmer for 2 minutes (you want them to be super-soft), then rinse under cold water to stop the cooking process.

Crush the garlic and anchovies together in a bowl, then whisk in Worcestershire sauce, lemon juice, olive oil and half the parmesan.

Place lettuce in a serving bowl, break open the eggs and scoop the soft whites and yolks over the top. Pour the anchovy and parmesan dressing over and toss well, seasoning with freshly ground pepper. Scatter with croutons and remaining parmesan. Purists believe this salad is best without any further additions, and we agree!

Steamed baby vegetables with gheeonnaise and lime

When the new-season baby vegetables begin to arrive through early spring and into summer, we like to cook them as simply as possible with a little touch to help us appreciate their goodness. Here the touch comes from making a mayo from ghee when it's still warm, basically creating a sauce that's halfway between mayonnaise and hollandaise. The way we like to serve this most is with an array of just-cooked baby vegetables. The most important thing is to get whatever looks good at the markets, but any combination of small turnips, parsnips, carrots, leeks, spring garlic, broccolini, asparagus, baby fennel, peas, beans and even lettuce all work amazingly well. If we have a selection we'll steam or simmer the vegetables that take the longest first, such as parsnips and leeks, then progressively add others to the pan, ending with those that just need a lick of heat, such as fresh peas. Once just cooked, simply drain and arrange them beautifully on a plate with a large dollop of gheeonnaise and a wedge of lime.

Serves 4

Baby seasonal vegetables, including turnips, parsnips, carrots, beetroot, leeks, spring garlic, broccolini, asparagus, fennel, peas, beans and lettuce
Lime wedges, to serve

GHEEONNAISE
1 organic egg
1 teaspoon white wine vinegar
1 sprig thyme or tarragon, leaves picked
1 small garlic clove
100 ml (3½ fl oz) Ghee (see page 227), still in liquid form

For gheeonnaise, place all ingredients, except ghee, into a jug and blend with a stick blender to incorporate (you can use a whisk, but a stick blender is far easier). With the blender running, slowly drizzle in ghee until creamy and emulsified. Adjust seasoning to your liking. Remember it needs to be kept at a warm room temperature to remain in its mayo-like form.

Steam baby vegetables until just cooked. Serve in a bowl or on a platter with the gheeonnaise and lime wedges.

Heirloom spring carrots with almond-tahini purée and coconut dukkah

If you can find good heirloom carrots then go for them, otherwise just normal Dutch carrots or young carrots will do for this dish. This works well as a simple individual dish, but we prefer to present it in one large platter on a sharing table.

Serves 4–6

2 bunches organic or baby heirloom carrots, scrubbed (skins left on if young)
2 tablespoons olive oil
2 handfuls wild rocket (arugula)
2 handfuls radicchio leaves, larger leaves torn
2 handfuls snow peas (mange tout)
1 tablespoon Coconut dukkah (see page 247)

ALMOND-TAHINI PURÉE
¾ cup (200 g) tahini
3½ cups (350 g) almond meal
1½ teaspoons lemon juice
1 garlic clove

GARLIC-MAPLE DRESSING
½ cup (125 ml) extra-virgin olive oil
2 tablespoons lemon juice
1 tablespoon maple syrup
1 teaspoon Dijon mustard
½ garlic clove, crushed

For almond-tahini purée, combine all ingredients in a blender with 400 ml (14 fl oz) cold water and 1 teaspoon salt and blitz until smooth. Season to taste. Keep refrigerated for up to 5 days.

Preheat oven to 220°C (425°F). Spread carrots on a roasting tray, drizzle with olive oil, season with ½ teaspoon salt and roast for 5-10 minutes until carrots take on a little colour but still have some firmness.

Meanwhile, wash and trim salad and snow peas. If snow peas are lovely, tender and young, simply slice them into thin batons that can easily be mixed through the salad (otherwise steam them briefly). Dry salad leaves thoroughly and mix with the snow peas.

For garlic-maple dressing, whisk all ingredients together until well combined. Season with ½ teaspoon salt.

Remove carrots from oven and allow to cool a touch. Spread almond-tahini purée on one side of a serving platter to form a bed for carrots, then arrange them on top. Dress salad with garlic-maple dressing, toss well, then transfer onto the platter beside the carrots. Sprinkle dukkah over the top to serve.

Buckwheat blini with fish roe and wasabi crème fraîche

It's hard to beat this as a little canapé for a gathering. You can also substitute smoked fish for the fish roe. The true blini recipe is made with some rye and yeast, but this is our gluten-free version that achieves the fluffiness by incorporating whisked egg whites. Everything here can be prepared in advance and assembled at the last moment.

Makes approx. 50 blini

2 cups (250 g) buckwheat flour
1 cup (250 ml) filtered water
2 organic eggs, separated
2 tablespoons coconut oil
  or olive oil
50–100 g (1¾–3½ oz) salmon
  or ocean trout roe
1 bunch dill, roughly chopped

PICKLED RED ONION
2 red onions, thinly sliced
¼ cup (50 g) rapadura sugar
2½ tablespoons preservative-
  free red wine vinegar

WASABI CRÈME FRAÎCHE
1 teaspoon lemon juice
1 teaspoon freshly grated
  wasabi root, if you can find
  it, or a preservative-free
  paste or powder (substitute
  fresh horseradish)
1½ cups (375 ml) crème fraîche

For pickled onion, place onions in a small saucepan, add sugar, vinegar and enough water to just cover. Bring to a simmer, simmer for 3–5 minutes, then turn off and allow to cool.

For wasabi crème fraîche, mix lemon juice and wasabi together, leave for 10 minutes, then mix with the créme fraîche and season to taste with salt. Keep refrigerated.

Whisk buckwheat flour and water in a bowl until well combined. Cover and set aside for 30 minutes or so (if you have some live yoghurt, a little whey or some loose cultured cream you could add a tablespoon and mix it through well to help with the activation of the flour, then cover and leave overnight or for at least 6–8 hours to improve both the flavour and digestion). Add egg yolks to the batter, whisking thoroughly, then whisk in 1 teaspoon salt (you may need to add more water – you're looking for a thick batter with a smooth, runny texture). Whisk egg whites to stiff peaks in a clean bowl with a clean whisk, then fold them through batter.

Working in four batches, heat 2 teaspoons oil in a large cast-iron or non-stick frying pan over medium heat. Dollop tablespoonfuls of batter into the hot pan, spacing them out so you can get as many in as possible without the blini islands joining forces. Cook for 1 minute or until bubbles appear on the surface, then flip and cook for another minute. Cool on a wire rack and repeat with remaining oil and batter.

To bring the whole show together, arrange the blini on a platter and dollop a teaspoon of crème fraîche mixture onto each one. Spoon about ½ teaspoon fish roe on top of each, follow with a piece or two of pickled onion and top with dill to serve.

Simple spring greens with seasonings

Sitting silently, doing nothing, spring comes and the grass grows by itself

– ZENRIN–KUSHU

A little dish to bring a little happiness. This can be eaten on its own just for the sake of it or included in a simple eating program to help soothe and reinvigorate the digestive system. In this age of endless cooking shows and magazines where everything seems quite over-involved or fancy, the simple things are often left by the wayside. Why on earth would you include simple steamed and seasoned greens in a cookbook? Well, why ever not? Of course you can prepare this kind of thing as part of a larger meal, but try it as a solitary bowl of food to be eaten as the first quality greens of the season appear in the markets. Maybe eat it by yourself, being mindful of its simple beauty and happy that spring is here and, wondrously, the grass grows by itself.

Serves 1

2 handfuls spring greens
   (young cabbage, broccolini,
   snow peas/mange tout,
   runner beans or the like –
   any one or a mixture will do)
1 tablespoon olive oil
1 teaspoon butter
Juice of ½ lemon

Steam greens in a steamer set over a saucepan of simmering water until just tender, anywhere from 1–5 minutes depending on what vegetables you use. Play around with the different vegetables, but whatever you choose you want to retain some texture – if you're mixing hardier vegetables with snow peas, for example, then throw peas in just for the last 20 seconds. Tip everything back into the empty saucepan, add the oil, butter and a pinch of salt, gently mixing to combine. Tip out into a serving bowl, squeeze over a little lemon juice, add a turn or two of black pepper and job done. Simple goodness.

Spring crudités with miso aïoli

Do not underestimate the potential of this dish. For crudités to work,
you need well-presented vegetables and good dips. The value in this kind of
snack is that you aren't filling yourself up with breads or processed chips or
crackers; instead you're enjoying the nutritional benefits of both the raw and/or
steamed vegetables along with whatever goodness is in the dip or sauce.
Here we're suggesting an unpasteurised-miso mayo, but you can use pesto,
hummus, beetroot or bean dip or a selection of all these. The beauty of this dish
is that it can be as simple as you like – at home with the kids, for example,
we just offer carrot and cucumber sticks with a mayo to keep the wolves
from the door – or you can craft a more elaborate offering. This kind
of snack fills a gap but digests quickly and easily.

Serves 4

Several handfuls of spring
vegetables, such as: baby
radishes; carrots, peeled
and sliced into sticks; celery,
cut into sticks; baby fennel,
cut into wedges; sugar
snap peas
You can also offer other
vegetables that have
been steamed for a couple
of minutes: cauliflower,
separated into small
florets; green beans;
broccolini; asparagus

MISO AÏOLI
¼ cup (60 g) unpasteurised
white miso paste (from good
health-food shops, and Egg
of the Universe)
½ cup (120 g) aïoli (see
page 230)

For miso aïoli, mix miso and aïoli in a bowl until thoroughly
combined. Transfer to a dipping bowl.

Prepare vegetables by washing, trimming and cutting to
similar sizes. Any hardier vegetables, such as cauliflower and
beans, may need to be briefly steamed or par-boiled. To do this,
simply put them into a steamer for a couple of minutes or drop
into boiling water very briefly before draining well, allowing to
cool and then arranging on the plate with all the other elements.

Serve with the miso aïoli in a dipping bowl.

Rice, Brazil nut and linseed sourdough bread

Baking can be a difficult skill, but this bread is seriously easy once you have your starter up and running properly. The recipe is our version of one from *Bread Matters* by Andrew Whitley, an incredible book if you're at all interested in bread and how it can nourish you when made the right way. This bread avoids baker's yeast and gets its interesting texture and high nutritional quality from linseeds and Brazil nuts. The sourdough fermentation process makes micronutrients more available to the body than in a fast, highly yeasted bread, so while this loaf may seem to take longer to rise, it's definitely worth waiting for. We've also found that this method works well with any number of combinations of the main flours or nuts included here. We often substitute chia seeds or sprouted buckwheat for the Brazil nuts, for example. The best way to approach this recipe is simply to start experimenting – we promise you will find the process incredibly rewarding in so many ways. If you're not already running a starter you'll need to get it going at least 5 days ahead (see page 80); you'll also need to soak your linseeds the night before.

Makes 1 small loaf

25 g (1 oz) linseeds (flaxseeds)

75 g (2½ oz) brown rice flour

20 g (¾ oz) cornflour
(cornstarch)

20 g (¾ oz) tapioca flour

10 g (¼ oz) buckwheat flour

⅓ cup (50 g) Brazil nuts,
chopped

1 organic egg

2 teaspoons apple
cider vinegar

1 teaspoon sea salt

1¾ tablespoons warm water
(30°C/85°F)

Olive or coconut oil, for
greasing and brushing

PRODUCTION SOURDOUGH

75 g (2½ oz) Rice sourdough
starter (see page 80)

70 g (2½ oz) brown rice flour

85 ml (2¾ fl oz) warm water
(approximately 35°C/95°F)

Soak linseeds overnight in 50 ml (1¾ fl oz) cold water.

For production sourdough, mix everything together, cover and leave in a warm place (as near to 30°C/85°F as you can manage) for 2–3 hours. The production sourdough is ready when it has risen appreciably (it may also rise then collapse; this is fine).

Mix all ingredients together, including soaked linseeds, with 150 g (5½ oz) production sourdough into a very soft dough with your hands or a large spoon. When combined, scoop dough into a greased loaf tin; it should come about two-thirds of the way up the sides of the tin. Cover and leave to rise in a warm place. It may take up to 5 hours, depending on the vigour of the sourdough and the temperature of the kitchen.

When loaf is fully proved, preheat oven to 210°C (410°F) and brush the top of the loaf very carefully with olive or coconut oil. This will give an attractive brown finish.

Bake for 30 minutes until loaf begins to shrink away from the sides of the tin. If you have doubts, insert a skewer into the middle. If it comes out clean, the loaf is ready.

Rice sourdough starter

To make the Rice, Brazil nut and linseed sourdough bread on page 78,
you'll need a rice sourdough starter. Brown rice flour is full of wild yeasts
and can generate a natural leaven in 3–4 days without difficulty.

DAY 1

30 g (1 oz) brown rice flour
40 ml (1¼ fl oz) warm water (30°C/85°F)

Mix flour and water to a paste, cover loosely
with a thin plastic bag and leave in a warm
place (around 30°C is ideal) for 24 hours.

DAY 2

Stir your starter well, then add:

30 g (1 oz) brown rice flour
40 ml (1¼ fl oz) warm water (30°C/85°F)

Stir well and cover as before. Leave for 24 hours.

DAY 3

At this stage, you should notice some bubbles in
the sourdough and it should have risen up and
then fallen back a bit. Refresh again by adding:

30 g (1 oz) brown rice flour
40 ml (1¼ fl oz) warm water (30°C/85°F)

Stir well, cover and leave in a warm place
as before.

DAY 4

By now you should have a sourdough that
smells nicely acidic and shows clear evidence
of bubbling. Stir in:

¼ cup (45 g) brown rice flour
55 ml (1¾ fl oz) warm water (30°C/85°F)

The creation phase is now complete. Use this
starter to make a 'production sourdough' when
baking a loaf of bread. Rice flours can be quite
volatile, so either keep refreshing your starter
by adding a little flour and water every day, or
store it in the fridge for up to 15 days.

Purple sweet potato and okra laksa with raw noodles

Noodle soups, in their many forms, are fun to make and satisfying to eat. This version happens to be vegan, with vegetable noodles offering a point of difference.

Serves 2

1 lemongrass stalk (white part only), roughly chopped
50 g (1¾ oz) ginger
25 g (1 oz) fresh turmeric
1 onion, chopped
60 g (2¼ oz) raw cashews, soaked for 4 hours, drained
1 long red chilli (plus small chillies to taste), chopped
2 teaspoons tamarind paste
1 tablespoon coriander seeds
1 teaspoon ground turmeric
1 teaspoon ground cumin
1 tablespoon coconut oil
400 ml (14 fl oz) coconut cream
1 purple sweet potato, peeled and cut into large dice
4 coriander (cilantro) roots
400 g (14 oz) okra, chopped
2 tablespoons sesame oil
1 lime
1 handful coriander (cilantro)
1 handful Thai basil
½ teaspoon each white and black sesame seeds

RAW NOODLES
1 daikon
1 zucchini (courgette)
1 carrot

Place lemongrass, ginger, turmeric, onion, cashews, chillies, tamarind paste and spices into a food processor and blend to a smooth paste, then add 1 teaspoon salt.

Heat coconut oil in a wok over medium heat, then add paste and stir for 1–2 minutes until fragrant. Add coconut cream and 600 ml (21 fl oz) water, bring to the boil, then reduce to a simmer.

Add sweet potato and coriander roots (bruise them before throwing them in) and simmer until softened, about 10–15 minutes. Add okra and cook, stirring occasionally, for a further 5 minutes until soup is thickened and okra is just cooked through. Remove from heat and check the seasoning – you want a balance of hot, sweet, salty and sour.

Meanwhile, for the raw noodles, spiralise daikon, zucchini and carrot (you should have about 2 large handfuls). Toss with 1 tablespoon sesame oil and the juice of ½ a lime, then mix through half the coriander and basil.

Ladle soup into bowls, pile noodles into one side, scatter with sesame seeds and remaining herbs, drizzle with remaining sesame oil and serve with remaining lime.

Rare goat rump with salsa verde

We've been eating more and more goat meat in the past few years, firstly because of its flavour – rich like mutton, but somehow cleaner than lamb – and how easy it is to cook, and secondly because of its low environmental impact – goats are able to graze on pastures that aren't suitable for sheep and cattle. Don't be afraid to ask your butcher to order you some. This is a perfect dish to try with our Salsa verde (see page 233), which has enough punch and acid to keep the richness in check.

Serves 4

1 tablespoon berbere
(Ethiopian spice mix;
from African grocers or
gourmet food shops)
1 piece goat rump (750 g–1 kg/
1 lb 10 oz–2 lb 4 oz)
1 teaspoon olive oil, plus extra
for drizzling
1 onion, quartered
2 carrots, roughly chopped
100 ml (3½ fl oz) chicken stock
(see page 234)
1 teaspoon quince paste
or jelly (optional)
1 teaspoon butter
Roasted broccoli, to serve
Salsa verde (see page 233),
to serve

Preheat oven to 200°C (400°F). Rub berbere onto goat rump, avoiding the fat cap, then rub oil and ½ teaspoon salt into fat cap.

Heat a large ovenproof frying pan over medium–high heat. Add rump, fat-side down, and fry for 3–5 minutes until nicely browned, then turn to brown lightly all over, about 2–3 minutes. Add onion and carrot to pan and toss to coat in oil and rendered fat (add a little more oil, if necessary).

Transfer to oven and roast for 15–20 minutes for rare. Remove from pan and cover lightly with foil to rest for 10 minutes.

As the meat rests, place frying pan over medium heat and add chicken stock. Scrape base of the pan to loosen any sediment, then add quince paste, stirring to dissolve. Add butter and stir until melted, combined and nicely glossy.

Slice goat (not too thinly) and spoon over gravy and roasted vegetables. Serve with roasted broccoli and salsa verde.

Raw caramel slice

This has been one of the more popular sweets at the café since the beginning. We've played around with it over the years to get the balance of flavour right so it's nicely rich, but not overly heavy on coconut oil as many raw desserts seem to be. This takes some time and effort so it's well worth doing a large batch and freezing the extra in slices.

Makes 30 bite-sized pieces

365 g (13 oz) coconut oil, plus extra for greasing
5 cups (750 g) raw cashews
500 g (1 lb 2 oz) date paste (or simply deseed and mash medjool dates)
100 g (3½ oz) tahini
400 ml (14 fl oz) brown rice syrup
100 ml (3½ fl oz) coconut milk
150 g (5½ fl oz) raw cacao powder
Chia seeds, to serve

Grease a 26 cm x 36 cm (10½ inch x 14¼ inch) slice tin and line with baking paper.

To make base, melt 65 g (2¼ oz) coconut oil over a heatproof bowl set over a saucepan of simmering water (don't let the bowl touch the water). Pulse cashews in a food processor until coarsely chopped (be careful, too much and it can become a paste). Place 250 g (9 oz) date paste in a stand mixer fitted with the paddle attachment and pour 100 ml (3½ fl oz) water over the top, stirring to combine. Add melted coconut oil, chopped cashew and a generous pinch of salt, then beat gently to combine. Transfer to slice tin, pressing the layer flat with the back of a spoon. Place tin in freezer for base to set.

To make middle layer, melt 150 g (5½ oz) coconut oil in the heatproof bowl as before. Meanwhile, combine tahini and remaining 250 g (9 oz) date paste in stand mixer, then pour in melted coconut oil, mixing to combine. Add 1 cup (250 ml) brown rice syrup, followed by coconut milk. Mix well. Once base layer has cooled, remove from freezer and spread this middle layer on top, smoothing it with a knife. Return to freezer to firm up.

Melt remaining 150 g (5½ oz) coconut oil in a bowl as before. Meanwhile, whisk raw cacao into 150 ml (5 fl oz) water in a bowl until smooth. Whisk in remaining 150 ml (5 fl oz) brown rice syrup, then melted coconut oil. Remove slice from freezer and spoon this final layer over the top, smoothing with a knife. Sprinkle with chia seeds and return to freezer to set, about 1 hour.

Once fully set, remove from freezer, gently tease whole slab from the tin and cut into squares or triangles.

Beetroot and purple carrot muffins

We like to play around with cakes and sweets that involve some vegetable elements, and purple carrots are especially fun to use for their beautiful colour. This most recent carrot muffin recipe by our chef Gabe is beautifully fudgy and has that little extra verve from the golden beetroot icing. No golden beetroot? Top it with cream or yoghurt instead.

Makes 16-18

1 cup (200 g) rapadura sugar

1 cup (160 g) brown rice flour

1 heaped tablespoon
  baking powder

1 teaspoon ground cinnamon

4 cups (600 g) grated
  purple carrot

2 cups (280 g) grated beetroot
  (beets), scrubbed, then
  grated with the skin on

¾ cup (180 ml) olive oil

3 organic eggs

Sumac or beetroot powder,
  to serve

Whipped yoghurt or coconut
  cream, to serve

GOLDEN BEETROOT ICING

200 g golden beetroot
  (beets), peeled

1 tablespoon lemon juice

50 g (1¾ oz) raw sugar

½ teaspoon pectin

½ teaspoon ground ginger

1 teaspoon ground cinnamon

For golden beetroot icing, cover beetroot with water in a small saucepan, bring to the boil, then reduce heat and simmer until soft. Cool, then purée with lemon juice in a blender. Transfer to a saucepan. Whisk together sugar, pectin and spices, then add to beetroot. Bring to a gentle simmer to activate the pectin, stirring occasionally. Cool to room temperature, then chill.

Preheat oven to 170°C (325°F). Whisk together sugar, rice flour, baking powder and cinnamon in a large bowl, then add carrot and beetroot. The sugar in the mix will begin to macerate the vegetables and draw out their juice. Pour the oil over this mix and gently fold it through.

Whisk eggs in a separate bowl, then add them to the batter and fold through until thoroughly incorporated. Once combined, transfer batter into lined muffin moulds and bake for 15–20 minutes or until a skewer inserted into a muffin comes out clean (or with only the merest hint of purple).

Top each muffin with a spoonful of golden beetroot icing, dust with sumac or beetroot powder, and serve with whipped yoghurt or coconut cream.

Happy biscotti with chocolate seaweed fudge frosting

You have to start this frosting the day before, but it's so good that it's well worth it! The measurements in this recipe count, so be exacting.

Makes 20

200 g (7 oz) coconut oil, plus extra for greasing
1 cup (250 ml) maple syrup
⅓ cup (90 g) tahini
560 g (1 lb 4 oz) almond meal
125 g (4½ oz) tapioca flour
¾ cup (65 g) desiccated coconut
12 g (¼ oz) sea salt
⅓ cup (50 g) white sesame seeds

CHOCOLATE SEAWEED FUDGE FROSTING
300 ml (10½ fl oz) coconut milk
3 teaspoons agar powder (from select health-food shops)
½ cup (55 g) raw cacao powder
1½ cups (375 ml) maple syrup
1½ tablespoons cornflour (cornstarch) or kudzu
1 teaspoon pure vanilla extract
100 g (3½ oz) dark chocolate, chopped into small pieces

For frosting, place 1 cup (250 ml) coconut milk in a saucepan and whisk in agar powder. Place over medium heat, whisking frequently. When mixture comes to the boil, reduce the heat to low and gently simmer for 1–2 minutes, whisking frequently, then shift to stirring frequently for 5 minutes. Remove from heat, whisk in cacao and maple syrup, then combine remaining coconut milk with cornflour, stirring to form a smooth paste, and whisk this into the saucepan to combine well.

Return the pan to the heat and bring to the boil, whisking constantly. The mixture will thicken and lose its cloudy look as it starts to boil. Remove from heat. Add vanilla extract and chocolate and stir until smooth. Pour into a bowl, leave to cool for 15 minutes, then press a piece of baking paper onto the surface and refrigerate for 1 hour or until cold and set.

Cut into pieces and process in a blender or food processor until smooth, silky and very glossy.

Preheat oven to 175°C (325°F). Melt coconut oil in a heatproof bowl set over a saucepan of simmering water (don't let the bowl touch the water). Add maple syrup and tahini, and stir to combine.

In a separate bowl, whisk together almond meal, tapioca, desiccated coconut, salt and sesame seeds. Fold coconut and maple mix through dry ingredients until well combined. Make sure the texture is consistent throughout. Roll into 20 balls and place on a greased baking tray. Flatten each ball. Tidy up the edges of each biscuit with a knife. Transfer to oven and bake for 15–20 minutes or until golden brown. Cool, then sandwich together with frosting.

Summer

element
fire

organs
**heart and
small intestine**

Characteristics of summer

When we lived in London, nothing felt better than a summer's day. Perhaps it was how precious they seemed as they couldn't necessarily be guaranteed, but on the days when it was warm, the city came alive – pretty dresses, picnic blankets, bikes galore, garden parties and a sense of celebration and joy.

· ·

These are really the main characteristics of summer. If we turn to nature for the cues, think of a flower in full bloom and the expression of beauty at its fullest. Ideally, the things we've dreamt up in winter and focused on in spring now come to fruition. We want it to be a time when we celebrate all we have through all of our senses. Walk barefoot on the grass, breathe in the air, smell the fragrance of the flowers. Take notice of the details of a morning, the vibrant light of the sky, or the colours around you, taste the flavours of your food and extract the greatest amount of pleasure from the activities you're doing. And cherish your friendships – this is the time of year to celebrate.

As late summer comes, we can begin to organise ourselves for the beginning of autumn and, beyond that, the rest period of winter. Late summer is the time of long, hot afternoons, warm sun and time spent with friends having fun. If there's a sense of balance in those few weeks, there'll be a noticeable feeling of ease and contentment within, wherever we are, with our bodies ready to be nourished in all aspects, from the food we eat to the company we keep. We feel full, grounded and earthy.

feeling
uplifted

joyfulness

Summer

celebration

outward-
looking

Emotions of summer

This is a time for relationships, intimacy and fun. We tend to be more outward during summer, spending more time with friends and more time outside in the warmth.

. . . .

That said, during summer it's also important not to abandon the pillars, such as yoga and meditation, that keep our inner world calm and help to nourish the heart. If we don't spend any energy on this inner life, we can also feel anxiety and panic during these months.

The warmth of summer gives us a chance to celebrate all life has to offer, to illuminate our inner world and those around us.

Foods of the season

Summer is the season that embodies the celebration of nature's bounty. With the warmth and movement in these months, we naturally gravitate to lighter cooking and simpler preparations, while the abundance of ingredients encourages a refined sense of luxury and inspires creativity in the kitchen.

. . . .

The summer offers a plentiful variety of foods and our diets should reflect this. Spices, hints of sweetness and a light touch with salt flow into a cooking style that is rich in energy and minerals but not heavy. Foods that feel naturally cooling, such as salads, baby young vegetables – either raw or steamed – sprouts and seasonal fruits, will help maintain energy, while spicy, peppery and pungent foods will assist in dispersing excess heat.

We gravitate towards freshness and crunch, with cos, endive and rocket (arugula) forming the base for salads, while cucumbers, carrots, beetroot (beets), zucchini (courgettes), radish and green beans are all suited to being served raw or lightly cooked. Garlic and spring onions (scallions) give bite and pungency. Fruits are numerous, and as well as enjoying the abundance of berries, we seek out juicy fruits that are full of life – watermelon, mango, pineapple, stone fruits and crisp apples.

To do in summer:
- ⟩ Stay hydrated by drinking quality water.
- ⟩ Eat cooling foods to keep the inner fire balanced.
- ⟩ Maintain a healthy flow of energy in the body with cardiovascular exercise.
- ⟩ Trust your intuition; let your heart lead and head follow.
- ⟩ Celebrate all you have created, all you have worked for, and your friendships; practise many moments of gratitude through the day.
- ⟩ Have fun. Carve out time to connect with friends and stoke the fire of the heart through meaningful connections.
- ⟩ Build and celebrate community.

Seasonal practice

We tend to be out more in summer. For us that means being at the beach, swimming, surfing and bushwalking. And with more time spent with friends and family, it's important to make sure you set aside moments each day to nuture yourself and enjoy your own company; this will nourish the energy of your heart and ensure you don't burn out.

....

With so much outward energy, it's vital to find enough stillness to soothe the heart, and rest the system. Poses for the heart and small intestine support balance in the heat of summer and help us rejuvenate and recharge. For each of these poses, find just enough sensation for it to be interesting and stay for anywhere between 3–5 minutes to allow for the greatest benefits. Gently rest between each shape, lying quietly on your mat or the floor for a minute or so before moving to the next shape.

- **Sphinx:** lying on your belly, prop yourself up on your forearms with your elbows just forward of your shoulders. Breathe gently into the curve of your lower back.
- **Butterfly:** sit with your feet together and slowly lean forward to a degree that suits you. You can support your neck or let it rest gently, depending on what feels best for you.
- **Twist:** hug your knees in and then slowly release them to the side, keeping your eyes and face looking upwards and twisting through your back, chest, abdomen and hips.

Simple gratitude practice

We start each day with a few seconds lying in bed thinking of little things we're grateful for. There have been times in our lives where this has been harder than others. But start simply and allow the tiny seeds of gratitude to infiltrate your experience. The more that we enjoy the little things, the small moments in life, the less pressure it places on the big things, the major moments.

....

This could be as simple as feeling gratitude for a delicious meal to come, the warmth of your bed around you, a roof over your head, the love of a friend or partner, child or pet. Notice how this begins to change the way you feel. Gratitude is so close to love in the way it's felt in the body and it has a profound capacity to change the way we feel. The more we feel it and see it during our day, the more we attract moments of joy into our life. We like doing this first thing in the morning as it seems to settle and ground us before we get up and begin the day in earnest.

Gratitude unlocks the fullness of life. It turns what we have into enough, and more. It turns denial into acceptance, chaos to order, confusion to clarity. It can turn a meal into a feast, a house into a home, a stranger into a friend. Gratitude makes sense of our past, brings peace for today and creates a vision for tomorrow.

– MELODY BEATTIE

Activated buckwheat granola

We've had a sprouted buckwheat granola on the menu at the café from day one. What was once a simple dish has now evolved into one served with poached and fresh fruit, cashew cream and nut milk, but you can still eat it on its own or as you would any normal granola, or sprinkle it on top of The love cup (see page 56). Be warned: it can become quite addictive!

Makes about 1.5 kg (3 lb 5 oz)

1½ cups (220 g) sunflower seeds

⅔ cup (105 g) pepitas (pumpkin seeds)

4⅔ cups (420 g) desiccated coconut

500 g (1 lb 2 oz) raw sprouted buckwheat (see page 66)

1 cup (170 g) raisins

425 g (15 oz) date paste (or simply deseed and mash medjool dates)

100 ml (3½ fl oz) brown rice syrup or maple syrup

Soak sunflower seeds and pepitas in filtered water overnight to activate them. The next morning, drain seeds and mix with coconut, buckwheat and raisins in a large bowl.

In a separate container, stir date paste with 1¼ cups (310 ml) water, then stir syrup through. Pour this over seeds and buckwheat, and stir until thoroughly incorporated.

Preheat oven to 80°C (180°F) fan-forced. Spread granola out on a lined baking tray. Place tray in oven to dehydrate for 12 hours or overnight (it should be completely dry). Allow to cool, then break up the larger granola clumps with a spoon.

Granola will keep in an airtight container for a few weeks.

Corn and kale fritters

As a gluten-free family, we're often denied the regular dishes that everyone else seems to enjoy – croissants, schnitzel, hash browns and of course that classic Australian brunch dish, corn fritters. On our journey with good food that happens to be gluten-free to honour Bryony and our coeliac daughter, Olive, we've reinvented all of these dishes. Not only do we think they taste better, they also feel better in our bodies, so it's a win-win.

These fritters are light and easy to digest, and make a great addition to our weekend brunch repertoire. A splash of hot sauce at the end will add a little kick. We normally serve these with classic smashed avocado, tomato salsa, some thinly sliced fresh or pickled jalapeño and a simple green salad.

Serves 4

130 g (4½ oz) kale, finely shredded

2 small–medium corn cobs, kernels sliced off

6 organic eggs, 2 separated

100 g (3½ oz) buckwheat flour

2 tablespoons ghee, coconut oil or olive oil, plus extra olive oil for drizzling

Smashed avocado, sliced jalapeños (optional) and a green salad, to serve

TOMATO SALSA

2⅓ cups (350 g) cherry tomatoes

½ red onion, diced

4 coriander (cilantro) sprigs, finely chopped

1 dried smoked chilli (such as ancho), soaked for 10 minutes in hot water, then chopped

For salsa, toss ingredients together and season to taste with salt.

Preheat oven to 100°C (200°F). Stir kale, corn, eggs, egg yolks (reserve the egg whites), flour, 100 ml (3½ fl oz) water and 1 teaspoon salt together well. Whisk egg whites to stiff peaks, then gently fold them through kale and corn batter. They'll deflate a bit, but the whites will help the fritters become nice and fluffy.

Heat a cast-iron frying pan over medium–high heat. Add half the ghee or oil, swirling to coat, then spoon in large dollops of batter. Fry for 2–3 minutes each side until nicely browned, then transfer to oven to keep warm while you cook remaining fritters.

Serve with smashed avocado, tomato salsa and a green salad drizzled with olive oil.

Boiled eggs and condiments

Probably one of our favourite breakfasts and one that, with simple variations, will keep you satisfied through many mornings of the week. With good bread and eggs, and a selection of additional elements, the foundation for the day is set and the world is put to rights.

Serves 2

4 organic eggs

2–4 slices good bread (sourdough, paleo or otherwise), toasted

Cultured butter, for spreading

2 tomatoes, either fresh (we like heirloom or a handful of cherry tomatoes) or oven-dried (see page 59)

1 avocado

Taramasalata or fish roe, fresh goat's curd and your favourite lacto-fermented pickle, to serve

Lemon wedges, to serve

Boil your eggs to taste – we always veer towards soft. There are several ways to do this, of course. We usually place the cold eggs in a small saucepan and cover with cool water, bring to a slow boil, and once the water is bubbling, set the timer for 3 minutes.

While eggs are cooking, assemble your other chosen elements on plates. Serve on toast with whatever combination of elements you prefer.

Perfect circle with activated crackers

This salad, combining a few of the key wholefoods techniques of soaking and sprouting as well as fermenting, emerged as one of the classics from when we first launched. Once everything is made it can be assembled in a flash, but it does mean making the crackers as well as the cashew cream, pesto, tahini cream and sauerkraut ahead. If you don't have these on hand, start this recipe a day ahead.

Serves 4

1 avocado, coarsely mashed

2½ tablespoons olive oil

1 tablespoon apple cider vinegar

2 carrots, grated

1 tablespoon black sesame seeds

1 teaspoon golden raisins, soaked in filtered water until soft

2 beetroot (beets), grated

1 tablespoon white sesame seeds

1 teaspoon goji berries, soaked in filtered water until soft

4 heaped tablespoons Almond-tahini purée (see page 73)

4 heaped tablespoons Savoury cashew cream with beetroot powder (see page 224)

4 tablespoons Activated cashew pesto (see page 233)

4 handfuls mixed wild salad leaves or rocket (arugula)

4 tablespoons Sauerkraut (see page 238)

4 tablespoons Kombucha vinaigrette (see page 227)

Activated crackers (see page 246), to serve

Season avocado with 3 teaspoons olive oil, 2 teaspoons apple cider vinegar and 1 pinch salt. Toss grated carrot with black sesame seeds and raisins in a bowl. In a separate bowl, toss beetroot with white sesame seeds and goji berries. Season both with remaining oil and vinegar, and season with salt to taste.

We like to present this like a yin-yang symbol, with swooshes of almond-tahini purée and cashew cream on the base, a scoop of pesto on one side, and a scoop of avocado on the other. We top these with the carrot and beetroot salads and a handful of leaves and sauerkraut. We then drizzle it with vinaigrette and serve with the crackers.

Pea and goat's curd tart

Harry's mum Helen was famous for her pea and goat's cheese tart. This is our gluten-free version with a modification or two, but it still pays homage to her creation. Gluten-free tart bases tend to be difficult to get right, but we found one similar to this in a Lee Holmes book and it's easier than making a traditional base. Much fun and happiness can be found within the casing of a good tart!

Serves 6-8

2⅔ cups (400 g) fresh or frozen peas

4 organic eggs

200 ml (7 fl oz) single (pure) cream

2 tablespoons mint leaves, plus extra to serve

1¼ cups (150 g) soft goat's curd, crumbled

PASTRY

3 cups (300 g) almond meal

100 ml (3½ fl oz) olive oil

1 teaspoon thyme leaves

Preheat oven to 180°C (350°F). Grease a 26 cm (10½ inch) loose-bottomed tart tin.

For pastry, place ingredients in a bowl, add 2 tablespoons water and 1 teaspoon salt and mix together by hand until a smooth dough forms. Roll out dough, then use it to line tart tin, spreading it over the base and up the sides with your hands. Chill for 30 minutes, then fill tart shell with baking paper and baking weights and blind-bake for 10 minutes. Cool tart shell to room temperature.

To make filling, blanch peas in a large saucepan of boiling salted water for about 30 seconds (up to 1 minute if they're frozen). Drain and rinse under cold water. Place eggs, cream and mint in a bowl with a quarter of the peas and half the goat's curd. Blend with a stick blender, adding ½ teaspoon salt. Scatter all but a handful of the remaining peas into the tart base, then pour over egg and cream mixture. Crumble remaining goat's curd over the top and scatter with the last of the peas.

Carefully transfer tart to oven and bake for 30 minutes or until centre is only just set (it will continue to cook out of the oven so don't overdo it). Allow to cool for at least 15 minutes before teasing tart from tin. Serve topped with extra mint.

Kale and cashew chips

Despite the fact that we know these umami-rich, satisfying and crunchy chips disappear almost as soon as we plate them up, we still never seem to make enough. We recommend making a double batch and hiding the second away for another time. Kale chips need to dehydrate in the oven overnight, and the cashews need an extra night to soak, so begin this recipe 2 days ahead.

Serves 4 as a snack

⅔ cup (100 g) raw cashews

1 teaspoon nutritional yeast

1 teaspoon mixed dried herbs or 1 tablespoon finely chopped fresh herbs

1 teaspoon smoked paprika

½ teaspoon sumac

2 bunches cavolo nero, stems of medium and large leaves removed

Soak cashews overnight in 2 cups (500 ml) water.

The next day, rinse them well, then transfer to a blender with nutritional yeast, herbs, paprika, sumac, 1 teaspoon salt and 90 ml (3 fl oz) cold water. Blend until combined and creamy, scraping ingredients down sides of blender.

Gently mix whole cavolo nero leaves through cashew mix. You want each leaf to have a relatively consistent coating of the mixture on both sides (this can be a little challenging, so don't be too fussy about it).

Preheat oven to 80°C (180°F). Spread leaves out on a lined baking tray, close together but not overlapping (as they dehydrate they will shrink away from each other); use a couple of trays if you need more room. Place trays in the oven and leave overnight to dehydrate.

In the morning, check leaves are crisp and dry, then allow to cool and store in airtight containers – quickly before you eat them all!

Foraged green salad

Much of our neighbourhood surroundings are covered in wild greens that, if you can be sure they haven't been polluted or sprayed, can offer an amazing bounty and a good excuse to go out hunting. If you live in the countryside, you'll probably know where to look, but wherever you live there's often far more than meets the eye. Try to engage someone with local knowledge and see what else is out there. You can also potentially propagate these greens in your own garden or windowsill planter box.

Often these wild foraged greens can have quite strong flavours, but this tends to reflect their nutritional value. Balanced well with other leaves and herbs, they can create something far beyond the ordinary green salad. Dandelion, for example, is super-bitter; sorrel has a great, potent lemony flavour, purslane – as well as being high in omega-3 – has amazing texture, and wild fennel provides young leaves and flowers to enjoy. Wild spinach, watercress and rocket (arugula) are all around, too, if you look for them. Many of these greens can be found wild, but they also pop up at local farmers' markets from time to time, so keep an eye out there, too.

This salad can be enjoyed on its own, but a simple poached egg and a cracker or a slice of bread turns it into something more substantial.

Serves 2

½ garlic clove, crushed

½ cup (125 ml) extra-virgin olive oil

6 cups mixed wild greens (such as dandelion, fennel, sorrel, purslane, spinach, watercress and rocket/arugula), washed well

Juice of ½ large lemon

Fennel flowers, to serve

Place garlic in the base of your serving bowl, add oil and stir garlic through (at this stage you can leave this for an hour or two until you're ready to make the salad).

Build salad into the bowl, starting with hardier leaves, then more delicate ones. When you're ready to serve, scatter ½ teaspoon salt over leaves and toss to coat everything in the garlic oil. Squeeze in lemon juice, then toss again, seasoning to taste. Top with fennel flowers to serve.

Chicken-liver parfait

Organ meats are an essential part of the wholefoods philosophy.
They offer great nutrient density and they're one of the keys
to help us live more sustainably.
Many people find organ meats a bit challenging, but for some reason
chicken-liver parfait seems to be the exception to this rule. If the livers
are sourced from birds that have roamed freely on pasture, they're
super-nutritious and can be even more tasty.

Serves 6-8

500 g (1 lb 2 oz) chicken livers
1 tablespoon olive oil
1 cup (250 g) chopped butter,
    plus extra, melted, to cover
½ onion, finely chopped
1 garlic clove, crushed
1 teaspoon thyme leaves
1 teaspoon sherry vinegar
1 cup (250 ml) single (pure)
    cream, warmed
Toast or crackers, lacto-
    fermented pickles and
    a green salad, to serve

Clean livers before cooking by trimming off all the sinew and connective tissue. This can be a fiddly job, but it's an important one as it stops the parfait from tasting bitter.

Heat oil in a large frying pan over high heat, add livers and fry, turning once, until they're beautifully browned on both sides but still very pink in the middle, about 2 minutes each side. Remove from pan.

Reduce heat to low, add 50 g (1¾ oz) butter, swirl to melt, then add onion, garlic and thyme. Stir until nicely softened and lightly browned, about 10 minutes.

Increase heat to high, return livers to the pan, and add sherry vinegar, stirring to deglaze the pan. Cover with a lid, reduce heat to very low and simmer for 2-3 minutes until livers are just cooked. Allow livers to cool in the pan, then transfer everything to a high-powered food processor. Blend, adding the remaining butter a little at a time, until smooth (alternatively, you can stop it earlier if you want a more rustic finish). With the motor running, pour in warmed cream until super-smooth. Season to taste with salt and freshly ground white pepper.

Transfer parfait to jars, ramekins or bowls, depending on how and when you are going to serve it. Once in place, smooth the tops and pour over melted butter to cover. It can now be chilled (although it's great served immediately while it's still warm). It will live happily in the fridge for a week.

Serve on toast or crackers with pickles and a green salad.

Whole roasted fish with sauce gribiche

Whether feeding two or the masses, a whole fish is often overlooked as an option. It's a shame, because not only are whole fish more affordable (especially if you then use the bones and head for stock), they're also super-simple to cook. Ask your fishmonger for a sustainably caught, seasonal option, ideally one that hasn't been farmed. We tend to choose snapper, barramundi, salmon or other seasonal fish. We like to serve this on a platter, or even straight from the foil, with a beautiful sauce gribiche, some greens and maybe a crisp potato or two.

Serves 2–6, depending on the size of the fish

1 whole fish (snapper, barramundi or similar; 1 kg/2 lb 4 oz for 2 people or up to 3 kg/6 lb 12 oz for 6 people or more), cleaned
1 lemon, thinly sliced
1–2 handfuls celery or fennel trimmings (depending on size of fish)
2 handfuls soft herb trimmings (such as parsley or dill), plus extra to serve
Olive oil, for drizzling

SAUCE GRIBICHE

2 soft-boiled organic eggs
1 tablespoon Dijon mustard
1 tablespoon lemon juice
1 tablespoon capers
¼ cup (60 ml) olive oil
1 tablespoon chopped flat-leaf parsley
1 tablespoon chopped dill or fennel leaves

Preheat oven to 180°C (350°F).

Score the fish in 4–5 cm (1¾ inch) intervals on the diagonal with a sharp knife. Line a baking tray with two sheets of foil, large enough to wrap the fish. Spread lemon, vegetable trimmings and herbs in the base and top with the fish. Drizzle with oil and season with salt, then bring the edges of the foil up and around the fish, folding the edges to seal. Bake for 30–45 minutes or until fish flakes away from the bone easily (adjust the time depending on the size of the fish).

Meanwhile, for sauce gribiche, break eggs and scoop yolks into a bowl, reserving whites. Add mustard, lemon juice, capers and oil, and whisk to create a loose emulsion. Stir herbs through, then roughly chop egg whites and stir through. Season to taste.

Remove fish from foil, being careful of the steam, and transfer to a platter (or serve it in the baking tray). Top with some herb trimmings for colour and serve with sauce gribiche.

Not-butter chicken with brown basmati pilaf

We created this version of the classic butter chicken as a way of exploring a lighter, dairy-free version. We prefer to make the dish using ghee, but if you need to be strictly dairy-free, use coconut oil instead. Yes, this dish is different to the original but it's still great, and even better after a day or two, so feel free to make it in advance. It also pays to start this recipe a day ahead to soak the cashews and the rice, if you like.

Serves 6

⅓ cup (80 g) ghee or coconut oil

2 kg (4 lb 8 oz) chicken thighs, bone in and skin on (use other cuts if you wish)

400 ml (14 fl oz) tomato passata (puréed tomatoes)

3 cardamom pods

200 ml (7 fl oz) coconut milk

Roasted cashews (optional) and coriander (cilantro) leaves, to serve

Lime wedges, mango chutney and lime pickle, to serve

SPICE PASTE

1 teaspoon garam masala

1 teaspoon ground turmeric

1 teaspoon ground cumin

1 teaspoon paprika

½ teaspoon ground fennel seeds

½ teaspoon ground coriander seeds

½ teaspoon fenugreek

½ teaspoon ground cardamom

½ teaspoon ground cinnamon

½ teaspoon cayenne pepper (or more to taste)

½ teaspoon ground black peppercorns (use Indian long pepper if available)

⅔ cup (100 g) raw cashews, soaked for 8 hours

1 onion, chopped

6 garlic cloves

5 cm (2 in) piece ginger, minced or finely grated

2 cm (¾ in) piece fresh turmeric, minced or finely grated

PILAF

2¼ cups (450 g) brown basmati
  rice (ideally soaked in water
  for 4–8 hours)
1 tablespoon ghee or
  coconut oil
1 onion, thinly sliced
½ cup (75 g) small currants,
  soaked in water until plump,
  then drained
Small bunch mint,
  leaves chopped
Small bunch coriander
  (cilantro), leaves chopped

RAITA

2 cups (520 g) natural yoghurt
1 Lebanese (short)
  cucumber, grated
1 teaspoon garam masala
Juice of ½ lemon

For spice paste, combine all ground spices in a small frying pan and dry-roast over low heat for 1–2 minutes until fragrant. Drain cashews and place in a food processor with onion, garlic, ginger, turmeric, ground spices and 2 teaspoons salt. Blend until you have a smooth paste, adding 50–100 ml (1¾–3½ fl oz) water to loosen, if necessary.

Melt ghee in a heavy-based saucepan over medium heat, then add chicken thighs, skin-side down, and fry gently for 5 minutes until golden. Turn and fry for a further 2 minutes to seal, then remove from pan.

Add the spice paste, allowing it to sizzle and bubble for 1–2 minutes but not catch and burn. You want the paste to take on a little depth of colour here. Stir in tomato passata, cardamom pods and coconut milk, then bring back to a simmer.

Return the chicken to pan, submerging it in the sauce. Cover with a lid, reduce heat to low and simmer very gently for 25–30 minutes until chicken is cooked through and sauce has thickened and darkened.

Meanwhile, for pilaf, bring a saucepan filled with plenty of water to the boil. Rinse rice well, then stir into water with 1 teaspoon salt. Bring back to a gentle simmer, stir rice to prevent it sticking, reduce heat to medium and simmer for 15–20 minutes until tender. Drain, return to pan and cover with a lid for 5 minutes, then fluff with a fork.

While rice is cooking, heat ghee in a small frying pan over medium heat. Add onion and cook, stirring frequently, until caramelised, about 10–15 minutes. Once the rice is cooked and fluffed, stir onion through rice, along with currants and herbs.

For raita, mix all ingredients well in a bowl and season to taste.

Garnish rice with cashews and coriander and serve with curry, raita and lime wedges. We also like to serve this with mango chutney and lime pickle.

Not-butter chicken with
brown basmati pilaf,
page 120

TEDx burger

We've always loved burgers, and Harry's dream day in Oz (pre kids!) was waking up and heading to the beach for a long surf, followed by a burger and rest time before returning to the surf in the afternoon, well fuelled and rested. The name for this burger came from Harry preparing for his TEDx Talk and looking for inspiration as to what to use as props on stage. The core concept of wholefoods is that many of our traditional dishes are perfectly healthy – if done well. There's nothing wrong with a burger if you're using good ingredients.

Makes 2

1 tablespoon olive oil

100 g (3½ oz) unpasteurised-milk cheddar (such as Bruny Island Cheese Co), sliced

2 wholemeal sourdough rolls, cut in half

Fermented mustard (see page 224), to serve

2 handfuls wild leaves (or rocket/arugula or cos leaves)

1 heirloom tomato, sliced

25 g (1 oz) Pickled cucumbers (see page 245), sliced

Mayo (see page 229), BBQ sauce (see page 225) and Sauerkraut (see page 238), to serve

BURGER PATTIES

300 g (14 oz) pasture-raised and finished beef, minced

½ onion, finely diced

1 garlic clove, minced

1 teaspoon Dijon mustard

2 teaspoons very finely chopped flat-leaf parsley

1 organic egg

For the patties, add all the ingredients to a bowl with 1 teaspoon salt and mix with your hands to combine well. Divide this mix in two and shape each portion into a large, flat patty.

Preheat a char-grill pan or barbecue grill to medium–high. Brush grill with oil, then fry patties on one side for 4 minutes or until nicely charred. Flip patties, then top with cheddar. Continue to grill for 4 minutes or until patties are nicely caramelised and cheese is softly melted. You still want the patties to be rare inside. Transfer patties to a plate and rest until ready to serve.

Place bread rolls, cut-side down, on the grill and grill for 2 minutes until toasted.

Build your burger by smearing mustard on the base, followed by leaves, tomato, then the patty. Top with pickled cucumber, mayo, BBQ sauce and sauerkraut. Finish with lids and attack immediately.

Macadamia lamington balls

This slightly more exciting version of a bliss ball borrows the jam
and coconut coating from an Australian classic, the lamington.
You will need a sugar thermometer for this recipe.

Makes 25

40 g (1½ oz) coconut oil

1⅓ cups (210 g) macadamia nuts

120 g (4¼ oz) date paste
(or mashed, seeded
medjool dates)

2 tablespoons brown rice syrup

1⅓ cups (120 g) desiccated
coconut, plus extra to coat

1⅓ cups (150 g) raw cacao
powder

1 teaspoon pure vanilla extract

RASPBERRY JAM

400 g (14 oz) frozen raspberries

5 g (⅛ oz) pectin

200 g (7 oz) raw sugar

Melt coconut oil in a heatproof bowl set over a saucepan of
simmering water (don't allow bowl to touch water).

Place macadamia nuts in a food processor or blender, and
blend for 5–10 minutes until a smooth paste. Add coconut oil and
pulse to combine.

Mix date paste into 200 ml (7 fl oz) boiling water and stir until
completely combined. Add to processor along with brown rice
syrup and mix on low speed until combined, then pour into a bowl.

Toast desiccated coconut in a dry frying pan, tossing, for
1–2 minutes until light brown. Remove from pan, then add to
macadamia mix with cacao, vanilla and ½ teaspoon salt. Divide
mix into 25 portions (approximately 35 g/1¼ oz each) and roll them
between your palms to make round balls. Chill.

To make jam, place raspberries in a stainless steel saucepan
over low heat. Whisk the pectin through the sugar in a small bowl,
then add to pan with raspberries and fold through – no need to
wait for the raspberries to collapse. Stir until sugar dissolves,
then bring the mix to 100°C (200°F) on a sugar thermometer.
Simmer for 5 minutes to activate the pectin, then blend well with
a stick blender. Transfer jam to a large bowl or a clean, flat baking
tray and lay baking paper on the surface. Leave to cool (the jam
will set as it cools).

Once jam is cool, roll balls in jam, then roll balls in extra
coconut to coat.

Trail 'bars'

Trail bars work all year round and can be re-imagined with all kinds of different nuts, seeds, spices and extras, such as goji berries, hemp seeds or even chocolate. This recipe, which is less bar, more biscuit – we like to call them Cockatoo Cookies – is an evolution of our original. They're a perfect snack in the lead up to a yoga class or training session – they'll give you a boost of energy to get you up into handstand or that last chin-up.

Makes 25

¾ cup (100 g) macadamia nuts
150 g (5½ oz) almonds
1 cup (145 g) sunflower seeds
100 g (3½ oz) pepitas
   (pumpkin seeds)
250 g (9 oz) pitted
   medjool dates
50 g (1¾ oz) chia seeds
50 g (1¾ oz) linseeds (flaxseeds)
50 g (1¾ oz) raw cacao nibs
150 ml (5 fl oz) brown rice syrup
25 g (1 oz) black sesame seeds
3 teaspoons pure
   vanilla extract
2 teaspoons ground ginger
1 teaspoon ground cinnamon
½ teaspoon ground allspice
½ teaspoon ground cloves

Preheat oven to 140°C (275°F).

Place macadamia nuts and almonds in a food processor and blitz for 30 seconds until coarsely chopped. Add sunflower seeds, pepitas and dates, then pulse for 10–15 seconds. Empty into a large bowl, add remaining ingredients and mix gently with your hands.

Place heaped tablespoons of mixture into muffin trays lined with baking paper, spreading the mixture out to fill just the base of the moulds; they should be about 3 mm (⅛ inch) thick.

Bake for 15 minutes until set, then allow to cool. Trail 'bars' will keep for 3-5 days in an airtight container, and in the freezer for 3 months.

Sugar-free banana soufflé

Soufflés are surrounded by mystique. No doubt if you are under the
employ of an exacting French-trained chef, there is a good reason for this.
Your career might depend on the height of your dessert! But these soufflés are
neither fancy nor difficult, and they taste great, so it really doesn't matter
whether you get them puffing up like 1980s cappuccinos or they end up a little
flat. As a sugar-free dessert, they are a genius idea and they work incredibly
well with any type of cream or custard. It's easiest to whip these up with a stand
mixer, but you can also use electric beaters or a hand whisk.

Serves 4

1 teaspoon butter, for greasing

3 organic eggs, separated

4 ripe bananas

⅓ cup (35 g) almond meal

1 teaspoon ground cinnamon

¼ teaspoon stevia

Cream, yoghurt or coconut
   yoghurt, to serve

Preheat oven to 200°C (400°F) and prepare four ramekins
by greasing them generously with butter.

Beat egg yolks, banana, almond meal, cinnamon, stevia
and ½ teaspoon salt in a stand mixer fitted with the paddle
attachment until well combined. Transfer to a large bowl.

Clean and dry mixer (be thorough), then fit it with the whisk
attachment. Beat egg whites to stiff peaks, then gently fold them
into the banana mixture with a spatula.

Gently spoon batter into ramekins, filling them to just
over the top edge, then place them on a baking tray and slide
them into the oven, leaving enough room for them to puff up.
Immediately reduce oven temperature to 180°C (350°F). Bake
for 14–15 minutes until nicely puffed up and golden, and only just
cooked through. Serve immediately with generous amounts
of cream or yoghurt.

VARIATIONS

Play around with these additions to the basic recipe:
- Add 1–2 mashed dates into the banana mix.
- Grate 60 g (2¼ oz) dark chocolate into the banana mix,
  then finish with more just as they come out of the oven.

Dandelion affogato with no-churn vanilla ice-cream

Let's be clear here. Making a dandelion affogato is a fun little twist – a caffeine-free take on a classic – but really it's still all about the ice-cream. We love traditional homemade ice-cream (or to be precise, iced custard, which is basically what it is) but we've never had a churner, so we developed this recipe to make our own. All it takes is a little patience and some lead time. Of course this works with bought ice-cream, but where's the fun in that? You'll need to start this recipe 8 hours ahead.

Makes 4

80 g (2¾ oz) roasted dandelion root (if you use a good-quality version, the end result is far more flavourful)

ICE-CREAM
1 cup (250 ml) milk
⅓ cup (75 g) caster (superfine) sugar
1 vanilla bean, split lengthways
5 large organic egg yolks
2 cups (500 ml) single (pure) cream

For ice-cream, combine milk, sugar and a pinch of salt in a saucepan over medium heat and bring to just below boiling point. Scrape in seeds from vanilla pod, then add bean pod. Remove from heat, cover and leave to infuse for 1 hour.

Whisk together egg yolks in a heatproof bowl. Bring milk mixture back to hot, then gradually pour a little into the yolks, whisking constantly to prevent curdling. Gradually pour this back into the pan, whisking to combine with remaining milk.

Place over low heat and cook, stirring constantly and scraping base with a heat-resistant spatula, for 10–15 minutes or until the custard thickens enough to coat the back of the spatula. Set a large bowl in a larger bowl of iced water, pour in cream, then strain hot custard into cream, whisking as you go. Stir over ice until cool, then refrigerate to chill thoroughly.

Tip this custard mixture into a metal bowl and place in the freezer. Every 10–15 minutes, whisk the mixture thoroughly. When it hits the texture you desire, it's all done. You can leave it frozen at this point (cover the surface with baking paper) or serve right away.

When you're ready to serve, make a strong dandelion brew, however you make your coffee, with 2 teaspoons root per person. Allow the brew to cool a touch, scoop ice-cream into cups or bowls and pour in an espresso cup of dandelion brew per person. Like coffee, dandelion is bitter, so it balances the ice-cream beautifully.

Autumn

element
metal

organs
**large intestine
and lungs**

Characteristics of autumn

The main lesson we can take from autumn is to let go. Letting go of what we no longer need in order for us to have the appetite and inspiration to carry on. After the heat of summer fades, the leaves begin to turn red and orange, then eventually fall to the earth to feed the roots for the following cycle.

. . . .

Autumn delineates the end of a growing season. It's where nature begins to turn inwards. After the outward focus of summer, which celebrates the abundance of what's been created and produced, there is a tendency to feel the need to rest. As a result, we're naturally drawn to focus our energy inwards.

Everything in nature that's healthy flows. There is creation and destruction, night and day, warmth and cold, growth and death. In autumn, the trees let go of their leaves without resistance, and the process allows for nourishment of the soil below; we too have to let go before we can take in new sustenance. In the same way that we have to exhale before we can inhale, we need to let go of the waste to become more receptive; shed what we no longer need so we can feel the fresh inspiration. Think of exhaling before breathing in cool, crisp autumnal air.

Autumn asks us to prepare for tougher, colder weather, and detoxification plays a crucial part in supporting the immune system and barriers. Immunodeficiency can be the result of the inability of the immune system to flush out toxins, or problems in the transport of waste materials; boosting the immune system can improve circulation of waste for disposal, and may help to eliminate toxins. The body is exposed to toxins every day, and the immune system is charged with sorting it all out – detoxification can help to restore a weakened immune system.

flexibility

courage

Autumn

adaptability

confidence

Emotions of autumn

When we are in balance, we can feel gratitude and personal confidence, courage, flexibility and adaptability, all of which are crucial for staying healthy during the winter months ahead. They prompt us to prepare for the possible challenges of winter, by completing unfinished projects and clearing away clutter.

Feeling emotions is nothing more than our natural human reaction to life. But when they become prolonged or blocked they can begin to have harmful effects on the energetic body. Autumn is a great time of year to start a stillness practice, be it yin yoga, pranayama (breathing exercises) or meditation. It is the ideal season to turn inwards for what we seek, building resilience and a source of energy in the process.

Foods of the season

Autumn is a time to cleanse and eat simply, to rest the large intestine and prepare for winter. The general cooking principle of autumn is to celebrate the abundance that is still available, while keeping our senses attuned to the needs of the body as the weather begins to change.

....

Generally, less raw food with more lightly cooked yet nutrient-dense foods are advised. As cooler weather arrives, you may move towards heartier soups and more slow-cooked stews, and include more wholegrains and legumes.

Foods that are pungent, astringent and sour stimulate the senses and contract our energies while protecting and purifying our bodies. Sour foods, such as vinegar, lemons and grapefruit, as well as more pungent ingredients such as garlic, ginger, horseradish, cabbage, turnip and radish, help protect and purify the organs as do mucilaginous (slippery and jelly-like) foods – try adding seaweed to your soups, linseeds to smoothies and making fenugreek tea. We also recommend lots of dark green and golden vegetables, which are rich in beta carotene and vitamin A; they are great for protecting the lining of the lungs and digestive system, while the chlorophyll and fibre content of leafy greens are fantastic for helping our colons to detoxify and regenerate good bacteria.

This season is focused on supporting and clearing both the 'Metal Element' organs of the lungs and the large intestine. In doing so, we encourage our body's ability to take in and absorb fresh energy through our lungs, while letting go and detoxifying by cleaning out and repairing our digestive system.

To do in autumn:
- Consider a cleanse and let go of any physical weight you don't want to take with you into winter.
- Meet up with anyone in your life with whom there needs to be healing, or write a letter to them and burn it to let the emotions out.
- Start your day with some deep breathing or pranayama and some steady walks, breathing in the cooler air and filling up on inspiration for the beginning of a new chapter.

Seasonal practice

Breathing techniques of pranayama, as it's known in Sanskrit, are very effective ways of transforming our energy levels and affecting the way we feel, energetically and emotionally. They're safe and simple ways to start your day and help to tone your lungs and detox your system. Remember to go gently – anything that uses force misunderstands the process.

Nadi Shodana: alternate nostril breathing

⌡ **How to**
Sit in a comfortable position and relax your belly. Bring your right hand to your forehead and rest your index finger and middle finger against your forehead. Rest your thumb and ring finger on your nostrils, where the cartilage ends. Take a breath out through both nostrils. Close your right nostril and inhale through your left nostril; at the top of your breath, close your left and exhale through your right nostril. Inhale through your right nostril; at the top of your breath, close your right nostril and exhale through your left. Continue for a few more rounds, finishing up with an exhale through the left nostril, then sit in stillness for a minute or two.

⌡ **Benefits**
Balances out the feminine and masculine channels or poles in the body: the yin and the yang. Helps to settle our nervous system and infuses the body with oxygen. Plus, it just feels good.

⌡ **Contraindications**
Don't do this if your nose is blocked or you have cold or flu. If your nose is blocked, you can practise instead using visualisation. It is best to practise on an empty stomach. If it causes anxiety or restlessness, return to normal breathing.

Kapalabhati breathing: skull polishing breath

How to

Sit comfortably. Relax your belly. If you're new to it, you can bring one hand to your belly to help you learn to contract just that part of your abdomen. You want to keep your shoulders relaxed and your ribcage still – it's just your belly moving in and out, like a pump.

Take a breath in and, as you exhale, focus on drawing your belly in towards the abdomen in quick, strong movements, as if there is a little cord attached to the inside of the belly that you're drawing towards the spine. Do this for a number of rounds; you could start with 20 or go to 40 and then sit and breathe normally. Enjoy the space you have created physically and mentally for yourself.

Benefits

Aids digestion and strengthens abdominal wall; tones and cleanses the respiratory system by encouraging the release of various toxins. It's very invigorating for the mind and helps to create a sensation of spaciousness in the internal body.

Contraindications

Don't do this if you're pregnant, or if you have stomach ulcers or high or low blood pressure. Avoid this if you suffer from glaucoma or have a history of heavy nose bleeds, or if you've undergone recent abdominal surgery.

Fasting

Many cultures traditionally have times of the year that are reserved for mindful or spiritual abstinence. Prior to the development of these cultural traditions, early agricultural societies would have had regular periods when many foods weren't available. As hunter-gatherers, we would have had enforced times of fasting and deprivation, which our bodies are well adapted to cope with.

The benefits of fasting are that they allow the body to clear out and clean the digestive system, and if this is done well, the result is a renewed sense of wellness. We find that regular cleanses and fasting are highly beneficial for our general wellbeing.

If you are considering undertaking any fast or cleanse beyond the simple routines outlined, consult a holistic doctor or practitioner. See page 55 for our fasting practice.

Mushrooms, kale and curd on toast

Mushrooms on toast is one of those things in life that just makes us happy. If you're lucky enough to come across some good mushrooms then, with a bit of butter, garlic and a hot pan, you can create magic. Our version includes the addition of kale and goat's curd, which all balances beautifully.

Serves 2

Olive oil, for drizzling

2 tablespoons butter

400 g (14 oz) mixed mushrooms (we generally use king brown and button mushrooms), sliced

1 garlic clove (half crushed, half kept whole for rubbing the toasts)

120 g (4¼ oz) kale leaves, coarsely shredded

80 g (2¾ oz) pesto (such as Activated cashew pesto, see page 233)

2 slices paleo bread (see page 155) or spelt sourdough bread, toasted

100 g (3½ oz) goat's curd

1 tablespoon Sauerkraut (see page 238)

Sumac, to serve

Lemon wedges, to serve

Heat a large frying pan over medium–high heat. Add oil to the pan and then butter. Swirl until melted, then add mushrooms, season with salt to taste and cook, stirring occasionally, until browned and tender but not completely soft, about 3–5 minutes – all mushrooms cook at different rates so a little experimentation here won't go amiss. When mushrooms are almost done, add garlic and kale and sauté for 2 minutes or so until kale is wilted.

Spread plates with a spoon of pesto, give each piece of toast a quick rub with cut garlic, then place on plates. Pile mushrooms and kale on top, scatter with goat's curd and sauerkraut, sprinkle with sumac and serve with lemon wedges.

Super BLAT

Those so inclined know that bacon tastes good. But good bacon – sustainably produced and cured using no nitrates – is even better. This has been our best-selling dish since it went on the menu back in 2013 and for good reason: the classic bacon, lettuce, avo and tomato combo is an all-time winner. We just make ours using high-quality produce along with house-made turmeric aïoli. These base ingredients, along with the addition of sauerkraut and the pickle-juice shot on the side to aid digestion, are what make this so super.

Makes 2

4 rashers nitrate-free, pasture-raised bacon

2 large slices good sourdough bread, toasted

½ avocado, either sliced or seasoned as per Avo-tomato on toast (see page 59)

4 oven-dried tomato halves (see page 59) or fresh (or fried in your bacon pan)

2 handfuls mesclun

1 tablespoon Kombucha vinaigrette (see page 227; or a drizzle of olive oil and a squeeze of lemon juice)

2 tablespoons Aïoli or Turmeric aïoli (see page 231)

2 tablespoons Sauerkraut (see page 238), plus ¼ cup (60 ml) sauerkraut juice to serve

Hemp seeds and sumac, to serve

Heat a frying pan over medium heat, add bacon and begin to fry, allowing the fat to render out and turn crisp without drying out the meat, about 5 minutes. There's an art to cooking bacon: there are many variables, including the cut of meat you are using and how it's been cured. Experiment with the heat and timing, and keep the fat in contact with the pan, folding the bacon over itself so the sections that don't have fat on them are off the heat and don't overcook.

Spread toast with avocado, place tomato on top, followed by bacon. Pile mesclun on the side, drizzle with a little vinaigrette, then drizzle aïoli over the whole show. Scatter with sauerkraut and serve with sauerkraut-juice shots on the side.

Sweet potato and buckwheat pancakes

This dish was originally created by Brendon Vallejo, one of our early chefs. We serve a single fat pancake with sweet potato and seeds to give it a nutritional boost that takes it far beyond the simple happiness formula of carbs, butter and sugar. Start this recipe a day ahead to soak the flours and seeds.

Serves 4

2¼ cups (300 g) buckwheat flour

⅔ cup (110 g) brown rice flour

1½ tablespoons chia seeds

2 tablespoons linseeds (flaxseeds)

¼ teaspoon ground cinnamon

3 organic eggs

1½ teaspoons baking powder

1 cup (125 g) grated sweet potato

⅓ cup (80 ml) coconut oil

Cashew cream (see page 224), to serve

Poached pears (see page 215), to serve

Maple syrup, to serve

CARAMELISED BANANAS

1 tablespoon olive oil

2 bananas, halved lengthways

1 tablespoon unsalted butter

Whisk together both flours, chia seeds, linseeds and cinnamon in a large bowl. Add about 3 cups (750 ml) water to the bowl – so that the mixture weighs 1.2 kg (2 lb 12 oz) in total – whisking and stirring the water through to create a thick batter. Cover and allow batter to rest and activate overnight.

When you are ready to make your pancakes, preheat oven to 200°C (400°F). Whisk together eggs and baking powder in a bowl and fold grated sweet potato through. Add this to soaked batter and combine thoroughly.

Heat a small, ovenproof frying pan over medium-high heat and add 1 tablespoon coconut oil and a large ladleful of pancake batter; this should immediately sizzle up around the edges. Cook for 3–5 minutes until the underside is nice and golden, then flip it, either with a flick of the wrist or with a spatula. Cook for 1 minute, then gently tease out pancake, transfer to a baking tray and place in the oven for 5 minutes until firm to the touch (you can start another pancake in this time). Transfer to a plate and cover to keep warm.

Wipe pan and repeat with oil and batter to make 4 pancakes in total.

Meanwhile, for caramelised bananas, heat oil in a separate frying pan over medium heat. Add banana, cut-side down, and fry for 3 minutes until golden. Add butter to the pan, allowing it to sizzle and melt, then remove from heat.

Serve pancakes with a generous dollop of cashew cream, caramelised bananas, poached pears and maple syrup.

Almost-French onion soup with homemade mustard toasts

This is a delicious and satisfying soup for the colder months. It also offers good nutritional protection against the elements – the addition of the ginger and turmeric serves to both fire up the digestive system while offering anti-inflammatory benefits. A winning dish to have on a day of simple eating. We prefer to have a denser, paleo-style bread on the side with a strong mustard to complete the picture. Yes, it takes time to peel and chop the onion and cook it gently for long enough to bring out its sweetness, but it's a dish of devotion.

Serves 4

¼ cup (60 g) butter

2 tablespoons olive oil

1.25 kg (2 lb 12 oz) onions, thinly sliced

50 g (1¾ oz) fresh turmeric, finely grated

75 g (2½ oz) ginger, finely grated

6 garlic cloves, crushed

2 teaspoons chopped thyme

6 cups (1.5 litres) chicken stock

4 slices wholegrain bread

Fermented mustard (see page 224), to serve

Heat butter and oil in a heavy-based saucepan over medium-low heat, swirling to melt. Add onion and a pinch of salt and cook slowly, stirring occasionally, for 10 minutes. Stir in turmeric, ginger, garlic and thyme, and cook for another 10–15 minutes until onion develops a bronze colour and is beautifully soft.

Add thyme and chicken stock, bring to a simmer and cook gently for 15 minutes until flavour melds and develops. Season to taste with salt and freshly ground pepper.

Toast bread and spread with mustard. If you don't have homemade, use a good bought wholegrain mustard.

Season soup to taste and serve in bowls with mustard toasts on the side.

Broth, sprouted buckwheat and greens with turmeric chicken

Once you have the basics of this recipe in the fridge it's super-easy to throw this together. It is both a simple cleansing meal and one that nourishes the soul when the winds begin to blow and the temperature drops. You'll need to marinate the chicken overnight.

Makes 2 large bowls

4 cups (1 litre) chicken stock
(see page 234)
¾ cup (140 g) cooked Sprouted
buckwheat (see page 66)
2 handfuls kale leaves, torn
Sauerkraut (see page 238),
to serve

TURMERIC CHICKEN

20 g (¾ oz) fresh turmeric,
finely grated
20 g (¾ oz) ginger, finely grated
2 garlic cloves, crushed
2 organic skinless
chicken breasts

For turmeric chicken, combine turmeric, ginger, garlic and a pinch of salt in a bowl to make a paste. Spread paste all over chicken and refrigerate overnight to marinate.

The next day, place chicken in a saucepan with enough cold water to cover by about 2.5 cm (1 inch). Place over medium heat and bring to a slow boil, then reduce heat to low and simmer for 15–20 minutes or until chicken is cooked through. Drain chicken, allow to cool, then shred with two forks. Chicken will keep refrigerated for 3–4 days.

Bring stock to a simmer in a saucepan. Divide buckwheat between two serving bowls, scatter a handful of kale around buckwheat and top with shredded chicken. Pour the steaming-hot stock over the top and serve topped with sauerkraut.

A kind-of paleo bread

The original inspiration for this recipe came from an event we hosted for Scott Gooding as part of his *Clean Living: Quick and Easy* book tour. In the pure paleo version there was no buckwheat and lots more nuts. Since this wasn't feasible in the café, and because we prefer breads that aren't so nut-heavy, we snuck in sprouted buckwheat, which helps produce a bread that's super-nutritious without being too dense. This bread freezes well, so we often make two loaves, slicing and freezing one to eat as we please.

Makes 1 loaf

1½ tablespoons pepitas
   (pumpkin seeds)
⅓ cup (60 g) sunflower seeds
1½ tablespoons linseeds
   (flaxseeds)
⅔ cup (70 g) almond meal
200 g (7 oz) cooked Sprouted
   buckwheat (see page 66)
½ cup (65 g) arrowroot flour
1½ teaspoons baking powder
5 organic eggs, beaten
¾ cup (125 g) firmly packed
   grated carrot
2 teaspoons apple cider vinegar
Coconut or olive oil,
   for greasing
Butter, to serve

Preheat oven to 175°C (325°F).

Place pepitas, sunflower seeds, linseed, almond meal, buckwheat, arrowroot flour, baking powder and 1 teaspoon salt into a large bowl and toss to combine. Add eggs, mixing well, then add carrot and vinegar and stir until thoroughly combined.

Transfer mixture to a greased 22 cm x 12 cm (8½ inch x 4½ inch) loaf tin and bake for 45 minutes until golden on top and firm to the touch (like an over-cooked cake). Remove from oven and cool in tin for 30 minutes before removing from tin.

Bread will keep for 1 week in the refrigerator or for a month in the freezer. Serve with plenty of butter.

Crab cakes with bitter-leaf salad and saffron aïoli

As well as the obvious appeal of the crab cakes, this recipe is another delicious way to enjoy a good aïoli, which, along with mayonnaise, is one of the best sauces to have in your repertoire. This recipe uses crab, but it's just as good with sustainably sourced, flaky white fish. If you do use fish, steam it gently over the saucepan of sweet potato until opaque and flaky, then cool before use.

Serves 4

750 g (1 lb 10 oz) sweet potato
(or Dutch cream potatoes),
skin on, roughly diced
1 garlic clove
1½ cups (250 g) picked crab
2 spring onions (scallions),
thinly sliced
1 handful flat-leaf parsley,
finely chopped
1 handful chives, thinly sliced
1 organic egg
1 tablespoon plain flour (or
buckwheat or rice flour)
1 tablespoon butter
2 teaspoons olive oil
Saffron aïoli (see page 231),
to serve

BITTER-LEAF SALAD
¼ cup (60 ml) olive oil
1 tablespoon lemon juice
½ garlic clove, minced
4 large handfuls bitter leaves
(such as radicchio or endive)

Place sweet potato in a saucepan with garlic and a pinch of salt. Cover with water and bring to the boil. Boil until soft enough to mash but still retaining some texture, about 10–15 minutes. Drain, then roughly mash with garlic. Cool.

Place mashed sweet potato in a bowl, add crab, spring onion, parsley, chives and egg, and season generously with salt and freshly ground pepper. Mix well to combine, then shape into 8–10 patties and dust with flour. Refrigerate for 20 minutes to firm up.

Heat butter and oil in a large frying pan over medium–high heat, add patties and fry for 5 minutes each side until golden and cooked through (you may need to do this in two batches).

For the salad, whisk olive oil, lemon juice and garlic together, season well with salt, then toss the leaves together with enough dressing just to coat.

Serve crab cakes with salad and saffron aïoli.

Kicharis

There is an almost infinite number of ways to make this Ayurvedic dish, but they all tend to riff on a concoction of lentils and basmati rice flavoured with spices. Kicharis is most often prepared with mung beans or chana dhal, but you can use other dhal, too. It's an ideal dish when you need a simple, nourishing meal. We season ours with black pepper, but if you can get Indian long pepper, it adds even more fragrance.

Serves 4

2 tablespoons ghee

1 teaspoon cumin seeds, plus extra fried in ghee to serve

2 teaspoons grated ginger

Pinch of asafoetida (from Indian grocers)

½ cup (100 g) red split mung dhal (or any other dhal)

½ cup (110 g) green lentils

1 cup (155 g) firm vegetables (pumpkin/squash, carrot, sweet potato), finely diced

½ cup (100 g) brown basmati rice

½ teaspoon each turmeric, garam masala, fennel seeds and coriander seeds

¼ teaspoon each fenugreek and mustard seeds

½ cup (25 g) spinach, chopped, plus baby leaves to serve

½ zucchini (courgette), diced

Lemon wedges, for squeezing

Raita (see page 121), Slow-fermented tomato chutney (see page 226), Sauerkraut (see page 238) and Coconut dukkah (see page 247), to serve

Heat ghee in a large saucepan over medium heat. Add cumin and ginger and stir for 2 minutes until fragrant. Add asafoetida, dhal and lentils, stir to coat, then fry, stirring occasionally, for 3–4 minutes or until lightly roasted.

Add firm vegetables, stir to coat, then add rice and stir again. Add 3 cups (750 ml) filtered water and remaining spices. Cover and cook over low heat for 45 minutes–1 hour, adding more water if necessary and stirring often to avoid sticking, until vegetables, dhal, lentils and rice collapse into each other and water is absorbed. Stir spinach and zucchini through the kicharis, season to taste, and turn off the heat.

Divide kicharis among bowls, squeeze over some lemon juice and sprinkle with extra cumin seeds fried in a little ghee. Dollop on raita and chutney, add some spinach leaves and sauerkraut and finish with a sprinkle of dukkah.

Power soup

This soup was first developed as part of a detox program we were doing, and has been a staple in our house for years. We were seeking dishes that left us feeling totally satisfied but could be made quickly and simply. The secret ingredients here are the unpasteurised miso and the umeboshi salt plum, which combine as a final seasoning to give an otherwise humble vegetable-coconut soup an umami lift. What's more, the chicken stock, seaweed and the raw egg dropped in at the end provide a real power boost to keep you energised.

Serves 2

1 tablespoon coconut oil

1 onion, sliced

400 ml (14 fl oz) can coconut milk or cream

100 ml (3½ fl oz) chicken stock (see page 234) or water

1 carrot, chopped

1 sweet potato, chopped

1 tablespoon dulse seaweed powder (from health-food shops, and Egg of the Universe; or wakame, broken up)

1 handful green beans, trimmed

¼ Chinese cabbage (wombok), shredded

2 bok choy (pak choy), trimmed

2 teaspoons umeboshi paste (or 1 umeboshi if you can't get the paste; from Japanese grocers or health-food shops)

2 tablespoons unpasteurised miso paste (we like the Spiral brown-rice version)

2 organic eggs

Heat oil in a large saucepan over medium heat. Add onion, stir for 1–2 minutes, then add coconut milk and stock or water and bring to a simmer. Add carrot, sweet potato and seaweed powder and simmer, stirring occasionally, for 10–15 minutes until vegetables are cooked through and quite soft.

Add greens in order of how fast they cook. First the beans, simmering for 2–3 minutes, then the cabbage and bok choy – we like them to be just cooked but still with some crispness; cabbage and bok choy can be added almost as you turn off the heat. Remove from heat to cool for 5 minutes.

While soup is cooling, spread umeboshi paste around the rim of each bowl. Add 2 teaspoons miso paste to each bowl and loosen with a splash of water. Add egg to bowls, whisk quickly with a fork, then ladle hot soup over the top and mix to incorporate; the hot soup will cook the egg. Serve immediately, adding more miso or umeboshi to taste.

Taramasalata with fennel and pomegranate salad

We wanted to create a gluten-free, low-carbohydrate take on this classic dip.
This recipe does the trick, and ends up with a beautiful texture, too.

Serves 4

3 small garlic cloves, crushed

5 spring onions (scallions), roughly chopped

35 g (1¼ oz) dried mullet roe (bottarga; from delis), thinly sliced

2 tablespoons apple cider vinegar

2 tablespoons lemon juice

1 cup (250 ml) olive oil

Toasted paleo bread (see page 155), sourdough and crackers, to serve

POMEGRANATE DRESSING

½ teaspoon Dijon mustard

¼ cup (60 ml) olive oil

½ teaspoon pomegranate molasses, plus any pomegranate juice from the salad

Pinch of sumac

Squeeze of lemon juice, to taste

FENNEL SALAD

1 small fennel bulb, shaved

2 handfuls rocket (arugula)

1 bunch watercress

Seeds from 1 pomegranate (retain juice for dressing)

Combine garlic, spring onion, mullet roe, vinegar, lemon juice and 2½ tablespoons water in a food processor. Blend on low to combine, then increase speed to medium and slowly add oil, little by little, until thick and emulsified. Season to taste with salt and refrigerate until ready to serve. Taramasalata will keep in the fridge for 3–5 days.

For pomegranate dressing, add all ingredients to a bowl, whisk to combine and season to taste with salt and freshly ground pepper, adjusting lemon juice to taste.

For fennel salad, toss fennel, rocket, watercress and pomegranate seeds together, then toss with dressing to coat.

Serve taramasalata with bread, crackers and salad.

Chicken marbella

This recipe is one of our favourites. Harry's mum Helen used to cook it all the time for big gatherings, first for the flavour, and second because it's so easy to make in advance and can be served at room temperature. We've rolled it out for many a party, including for the celebration the day after our wedding, and for Bryony's 40th. It originated in the seminal 1980s *Silver Palate* cookbook written by Julee Rosso and Sheila Lukins; this is our slightly adjusted version. It is almost essential to start this the day before, as you want it to marinate as long as possible.

Serves 10–12

1 cup (200 g) pitted prunes, roughly chopped

1 cup (125 g) pitted green olives, roughly chopped

½ cup (80 g) capers in vinegar (with a big splash of the vinegar), roughly chopped

6 large garlic cloves

3 tablespoons dried oregano

5 bay leaves

½ cup (125 ml) good red wine vinegar

2 whole organic chickens, jointed, with breasts cut into 2–3 pieces (or 12 marylands)

½ cup (105 g) rapadura sugar

1 cup (250 ml) white wine or chicken stock

1 handful chopped flat-leaf parsley

Combine prunes, olives, capers, garlic, oregano, bay leaves and vinegar in a large bowl with 1 teaspoon salt (taste the marinade; if it's not salty enough, add a little more salt). Add chicken and mix well, massaging the marinade into the flesh. Cover and refrigerate for at least 12 hours to marinate, ideally giving it a mix after 6 hours.

Preheat oven to 180°C (350°F) and spread chicken, skin-side up, on two baking trays, leaving room between each piece so it roasts evenly (it's best to keep the breast pieces together). Sprinkle each piece of chicken with a pinch of rapadura, then splash wine or stock around the chicken.

Roast, placing the tray with the breast pieces on the lower shelf, for 45 minutes or until the chicken is golden and cooked through but still juicy (it's ready when the juices run clear when a thigh is pierced with a skewer).

Either serve straight from the baking trays or transfer to serving platters, but be sure to scatter parsley over for good effect.

A NOTE TO THE COOK:

Don't let anyone throw away their bones. At the end of the party, deglaze the baking dishes and pour the juices into a stockpot, then add the leftover bones. This will create the best stock, that will bring happiness long after the last of the chicken has been consumed.

Roast beets with cucumber and goat's curd

A salad that shines on its own or as part of a selection of different salads for a dinner party. You can prepare the base of this dish well in advance, but it presents best if the final mixing happens just before you eat.

Serves 4–6

2 bunches beetroot (beets), scrubbed (peeled if the beetroot are older) and cut into wedges

Olive oil, for drizzling

2 small Lebanese (short) cucumbers, cut into ribbons (we use a peeler)

1 bunch dill, roughly chopped

¾ cup (90 g) crumbled soft goat's curd or feta

2 teaspoons nigella seeds

Preheat oven to 180°C (350°F). Add beetroot to a large baking tray or two (they shouldn't be crowded), drizzle with oil, season with 1 teaspoon salt and toss to coat. Roast for 30–40 minutes or until tender and caramelised. Cool to room temperature.

Layer beetroot, cucumber and half the dill, goat's curd or feta and nigella seeds in a large serving bowl and season with salt and freshly ground pepper. When ready to serve, toss the salad together and finish with the last of the dill, goat's curd or feta and nigella seeds.

Mushroom pâté

A dip or a first course for whenever you happen to have an excess of mushrooms and you feel like something a little special (that just happens to be vegan). This is great served on crackers or toast, accompanied by a fresh green salad.

Serves 4

¾ cup (160 ml) olive oil,
  plus extra for covering
1 onion, finely diced
3 garlic cloves
1 cup (20 g) dried mixed
  mushrooms, soaked in
  boiling water for 10 minutes
6 thyme sprigs, leaves picked
250 g (9 oz) mixed mushrooms
  (we use king browns and
  large portobellos), roughly
  chopped
1 teaspoon truffle-infused
  olive oil
Finely grated zest of 1 lemon
½ cup (60 g) walnuts
  (preferably soaked for
  6–8 hours in filtered water)

Heat 2 tablespoons oil in a large frying pan over medium–low heat, add onion and garlic, and fry, stirring occasionally, for 10 minutes until softened and lightly caramelised. Drain soaked mushrooms, reserving liquid, then roughly chop and add to the pan with thyme. Stir for 1–2 minutes, then add soaking liquid and simmer until evaporated. Remove from heat and set aside.

Heat 2 tablespoons oil in a separate large frying pan over high heat and add fresh mushrooms. Fry, tossing occasionally, until nicely browned but not completely softened, about 5 minutes. Add onion mixture to the pan, season to taste with salt and freshly ground pepper, and add truffle oil and half the lemon zest.

Spoon two-thirds of mushroom mixture into a food processor, add walnuts (drained if you soaked them) and blend until smooth, slowly adding ½ cup (125 ml) filtered water and the remaining ⅓ cup (80 ml) oil until you have a thick mushroom paste with some textured graininess to it.

Add remaining mushrooms and zest and pulse to just integrate the mushrooms. Spoon mushroom pâté into ramekins or small bowls and cover with a slick of olive oil. Refrigerate until ready to serve.

Rosemary and poppyseed oat bars

We created this recipe to commemorate the Anzac Day public holiday in Australia. The symbolic rosemary and poppy seeds transform what would otherwise be a standard oat bar.

Makes 10 bars

750 g (1 lb 10 oz) oats

½ cup (75 g) sunflower seeds

75 g (2½ oz) desiccated coconut

375 g (13 oz) butter, at room temperature

1⅓ cups (250 g) raw sugar

4 rosemary sprigs, leaves finely chopped

100 g (3½ oz) dark chocolate, coarsely chopped

Poppy seeds, for sprinkling

Preheat oven to 175°C (325°F) and line a baking tray with baking paper. Combine oats, sunflower seeds and coconut with 1 teaspoon salt in a bowl.

Beat butter, sugar and rosemary in a stand mixer (or by hand) until pale and creamy. Add butter mixture to oat mixture, and beat until well combined. Turn out onto the lined tray and press flat with the back of a spoon. Before you bake it, make indents into the surface of the slice with the back of a knife, pressing firmly to mark where you'll cut it once baked. These will be your bars. We like to cut it into 10-15 bars, but you can make more (smaller) bars if you wish.

Bake for 15 minutes or until light golden (the bars will start to crumble if you leave them too long in the oven, so try to catch them before they turn dark brown).

Meanwhile, melt chocolate in a heatproof bowl over a saucepan of simmering water (don't let the bowl touch the water).

Remove tray from oven and cut along the lines immediately to make bars. Drizzle melted chocolate across the whole tray of cooling bars, then scatter with poppy seeds. Cool, then store in an airtight container. Bars will keep, refrigerated, for up to a week.

Coconut matcha muffins

If you are into green tea, try these – they are really good. The matcha muffin with the Japanese green tea jam make a unique and fun combination.

Makes 18 muffins

175 g (6 oz) coconut oil

30 g (1 oz) chia seeds

275 ml (9¾ oz) coconut milk, at room temperature

1⅓ cups (120 g) desiccated coconut, plus extra to serve

¾ cup (125 g) brown rice flour

2⅔ cups (275 g) almond meal

75 g (2½ oz) rapadura sugar

½ cup (100 g) raw sugar

20 g (¾ oz) matcha powder

20 g (¾ oz) baking powder

75 ml (2¼ fl oz) olive oil

JAM

50 g (1¾ oz) desiccated coconut

75 ml (2¼ oz) 'vintage' kombucha (liquid from a jar of kombucha with a SCOBY)

2 tablespoons genmaicha tea

1 teaspoon matcha powder

75 g (2½ oz) raw sugar

Preheat oven to 175°C (325°F). Melt coconut oil in a heatproof bowl set over a saucepan of simmering water.

Whisk the chia seeds into the coconut milk and leave for 5–10 minutes to activate – they'll plump up and turn gel-like.

Dry-roast the desiccated coconut in a large frying pan over medium heat, tossing for 2–3 minutes until light golden. Transfer to a bowl immediately to stop it burning.

Whisk flour, almond meal, both sugars, matcha and baking powder together in a large bowl. Stir olive oil and melted coconut oil together, then whisk them into the flour mixture. Fold in chia seed and coconut milk, then toasted coconut, and stir until thoroughly combined.

Transfer batter into lined muffin moulds. Bake for 15 minutes or until a skewer inserted into a muffin comes out clean. Cool to room temperature, then remove the muffins from their moulds.

To make the jam, dry-roast the coconut in a large frying pan over medium heat, tossing for 2–3 minutes until light golden. Pour kombucha into the pan, whisk in genmaicha and matcha, then sugar, whisking to dissolve sugar. Bring to the boil, then pour into a baking dish, lay a sheet of baking paper on the surface and leave to cool. The jam will thicken as it cools. Once cool, spread onto the muffins and top with a little coconut.

Espresso-choc cardamom cake with coffee-cardamom ganache

A deeply rich cake with interesting spicing, this will satisfy
the most discerning of chocolate lovers.

Serves 12

175 g (6 oz) coconut oil,
    plus extra for greasing
⅔ cup (100 g) chopped
    dark chocolate
30 g (1 oz) chia seeds
1 cup (250 ml) coconut milk
¾ cup (125 g) brown rice flour
2⅔ cups (275 g) almond meal
¾ cup (150 g) rapadura sugar
100 g (3½ oz) raw sugar
20 g (¾ oz) baking powder
75 g (2½ oz) raw cacao powder
1 teaspoon ground cardamom
⅓ cup (80 ml) olive oil
200 ml (7 fl oz) espresso
Coffee beans, to serve

GANACHE

275 g (9¾ oz) dark chocolate,
    chopped
100 g (3½ oz) coconut oil
100 ml (3½ fl oz) olive oil
20 g (¾ oz) coffee beans
2 teaspoons cardamom pods

Preheat oven to 170°C (325°F). Line the base of a 20–25 cm
(8–10 inch) round cake tin with baking paper, brushing the
sides with coconut oil.

Combine coconut oil and chocolate in a heatproof bowl
set over a saucepan of simmering water (don't let the bowl touch
the water) and stir until melted and combined.

In a separate bowl, whisk chia seeds into coconut milk and
leave at room temperature for 5–10 minutes to activate.

Whisk flour, almond meal, sugars, baking powder, cacao
and cardamom in a large bowl to combine. Pour in melted
chocolate mixture, add olive oil and espresso, then gently
fold in chia mixture, stirring until just combined.

Pour batter into prepared cake tin and bake for 50 minutes
or until a skewer inserted into the centre of the cake withdraws
clean. Remove, allow to cool, then chill for 30–40 minutes while
you make the frosting.

For ganache, melt ingredients in a heatproof bowl set
over a saucepan of simmering water, leaving to infuse for
1–2 minutes. Transfer to a blender or food processor and blitz
for 1–2 minutes until combined, then pass through a fine sieve
and cool to room temperature.

Ice the top of the cake with ganache. It will begin to solidify
once it touches the chilled cake, so move swiftly to get the ganache
dribbling over the edges. The cake will keep in an airtight
container for 3–5 days. Serve topped with coffee beans.

Winter

element
water

organs
**kidneys and
bladder**

Characteristics of winter

Winter is when nature takes its deepest rest. Imagine the seeds of a plant lying dormant beneath the surface of the earth, waiting patiently and listening for the cues of the warmer months. The blankets of snow or patterns of frost over the earth, the darker mornings, the colder nights – all these point to the metaphoric sleep of winter.

It's also a time of year for us to rest and look inwards. Throughout history humans have allowed winter to be a time where we hold reverence and respect for this inward journey. It can be a time where we take care of ourselves, listen to the call of our soul and quietly make plans for the spring. That way, when spring comes, we will have the natural energy that comes with it.

The sleep of winter is the end of the seasonal cycle. There is work going on but it's more internalised and less obvious; it's a time of storing our energy. We can often try to fight against winter and just keep going at the pace we're used to, but it's the perfect time to surrender. It's not the time of year to sweat lots as the body wants to conserve water, so consider adjusting your yoga or other exercise rhythms accordingly.

gentleness

wisdom

Winter

openness

wellbeing

Emotions of winter

When we are in balance we can tap into our innate gentleness, wisdom, openness and an overall ease of being. When out of balance we can feel fear and sadness. The fear of letting go, fear of change and lacking trust not only in ourselves but also in other people or life.

. . . .

Winter is a time to look back at all that has been, to let go of what no longer serves us and to clarify what it is we want to manifest in future months. It's the time of year to do less and to say no to more, to go to bed earlier and enjoy more rest. It's an opportunity to nurture yourself.

Many cultures mark the darkest time of winter with festivals that both honour the darkness and also celebrate the coming of the light. This is a time to retreat into the darker months and then turn towards the light of the new season. The more we rest in winter, the more ready for the new cycle of spring we feel. With this appreciation for winter it becomes easier to yield to all the invitations the season has to offer.

Foods of the season

Winter foods are all about a deep sense of nurturing that will help us build and maintain our inner energies. Slow-cooked, warm, hearty dishes, such as soups, stews, broths and stocks, come to the fore along with wholegrains, legumes, nuts and seeds.

· ·

Dark winter greens and seaweeds help to fortify the kidneys, while seasonal vegetables in colours from yellow through to orange and purple tend to be rich in vitamin A and beta carotene to support our immune system. We're seeking to focus on highly nutritious foods that digest easily, and strike a balance between saltiness and bitterness to both direct our energies inwards and stimulate digestion.

We tend to find ourselves craving dark, leafy greens such as kale, Swiss chard, Tuscan cabbage and Brussels sprouts, as well as orange and purple root vegetables, including heirloom carrots, turnips, beetroot and sweet potato. Our salads take a bitter turn with radicchio, chicory, endive and celery. Winter is also a time to enjoy nuts and seeds, such as quinoa, amaranth, Brazil nuts and walnuts. For fruit, we look to good, seasonal apple varieties as well as avocados and citrus, particularly grapefruit.

To do in winter:

- Rest more, take time to recharge.
- Sleep in whenever possible.
- Allow yourself to be more introspective and to dream.
- Make more time for your inner life.
- Eat warming foods.
- Gather with those who mean most to you.
- Practise self-acceptance.
- Nurture yourself.
- Take time to clarify your vision for yourself so that when spring comes there is focus.
- Keep your kidneys warm.

Seasonal practice

Meditation has a long list of benefits, from lowering stress levels and blood pressure, to improving creativity and immunity and helping with anxiety and sleeplessness. While all these aspects are worthwhile, we like it for its ability to help us see ourselves more clearly, and to transform ourselves, as well as being a buffer against the intensity of life and a ballast to help us through each day.

Winter is an amazing time to dive into a meditation practice. It's the season that, above all others, has a mood of turning inwards. In meditating, we are creating a container for ourselves where we are able to hold space for whatever mood or mind state we are in. We are offering unconditional kindness towards ourselves, whatever the internal state is, neither antagonising nor deserting ourselves as we notice the mind often flinging itself from the past or the future or a running commentary on the present. We can remind ourselves to come back to the breath and return again and again to the now. As we say, using your mind to bring you gently back to a place of no mind. Our meditation practice has to be a friendly place or we won't feel welcome to begin again and again. Try easy exercises, come as you are and be patient with yourself.

Tips

- Set a timer so you don't have to keep checking your clock.
- Sit comfortably; it doesn't have to be in any particular position, just supported and easeful. This could be on a cushion on the floor, or the couch or a chair.
- Try to avoid lying down as it's too easy to fall asleep.
- You can meditate any time of day. For many, the first part of the day before the busyness begins will be best, while for others the end of the day may be most peaceful.

Breath awareness and breath counting

This meditation aims to train the mind towards single-pointed focus. It's a great way to begin to narrow your attention to your breath, cultivate awareness and to focus your mind.

It's simple, but no one ever said simple was easy, right? Keep it light and without seriousness. Trust that through learning to sit still and resting into our own company, the rest begins to happen on its own.

- Get comfortable, take a few deep breaths and begin to let go.
- As you inhale, simply feel the breath at the nose, the quality of the breath, the length of the breath, the sensation of breathing.
- At the end of the exhale, silently count to yourself: one.
- As you inhale, feel the breath as a physical phenomenon, notice the length and depth of the breath. As you exhale, count two.
- As you inhale, feel the air as it moves into the body via the nostrils. On the exhale, silently and to yourself, count three. Carry on inhaling and exhaling until you get to 10.
- If you get to 10, you can then count back to one.
- If you drift off, begin again at one.
- If you get distracted, begin again at one.
- If you notice yourself being able to count and think at the same time, concentrate more on the physical sensation of breathing and know that when we are truly feeling, whole-body feeling, we can't think at the same time.
- Give yourself to the physicality of breathing.

Winter breakfast bowl

This dish was inspired by bubble and squeak, the ubiquitous 'fridge scraps' dish in which you fry up leftover vegetables. We originally brought this bowl onto the winter menu and called it the 'Winter Breakfast'. It's nutritionally great for winter as the orange root vegetables are rich in vitamin A and the chlorophyll-rich greens support immunity through the colder months. As that first winter came to an end, the dish had a following and we weren't allowed to remove it from the menu, so it became the 'Spring Breakfast'. At the end of spring it became the 'Seasonal Breakfast' – and that's how it's stayed ever since. So while it belongs in winter, it can be loved all year round! You can make an ad hoc version of this breakfast with any leftover roast root vegetables. This is how we currently do it in the café, but feel free to improvise.

Serves 2

1 tablespoon olive oil

125 g (4½ oz) each roast sweet potato and carrots, chopped

150 g (5½ oz) kale, trimmed

1 tablespoon butter

2 organic eggs, poached or fried (it's up to you)

1 handful rocket (arugula)

¼ cup (60 g) Turmeric aïoli (see page 231)

2 tablespoons Sauerkraut (see page 238)

2 teaspoons za'atar or Coconut dukkah (see page 247)

SWEET POTATO PURÉE

1 large sweet potato

¼ teaspoon ground turmeric

½ teaspoon smoked paprika

¼ teaspoon ground ginger

1 tablespoon lemon juice

For sweet potato purée, preheat oven to 180°C (350°F) and bake potato for 45 minutes or until the skin blisters and blackens a touch, and the flesh is tender. Cool, then spoon flesh from skin and mash with a fork, adding spices and seasoning with lemon juice and salt to taste.

Heat oil in a large frying pan over medium-low heat, add roast sweet potato and carrot, and fry gently, stirring occasionally, to reheat. Add kale and butter, increase heat to high and fry, tossing gently, for 2–3 minutes until kale is softened. The trick is to have the roast vegetables reheated but not falling apart.

Spread a generous dollop of sweet potato purée on the base of bowls, pile in vegetables and kale, place eggs on top, scatter with rocket and finish with aïoli, sauerkraut and za'atar or dukkah.

Simple cleansing green breakfast broth

Our whole family loves this as a foundational start to the day through all of autumn and winter. If you're in the process of cleansing or fasting, this is a perfect way to help support your digestive system with simple nourishment. There are endless variations depending on the greens and herbs you use and the balance of flavours in your base stock. To boost this into a more complete breakfast, serve it with a poached egg dropped in and a side of sourdough toast.

Serves 4

1 tablespoon olive oil

1 thumb-sized piece ginger, finely grated

½ thumb-sized piece fresh turmeric, finely grated

2 garlic cloves, finely grated

2 spring onions (scallions), white parts thinly sliced, green parts sliced separately, to serve

4 cups (1 litre) chicken stock (see page 234)

2 handfuls green leaves (silverbeet, kale, spinach, rocket/arugula or lettuce; we like to reserve the outer scrappy leaves of lettuces just for this), shredded, torn or chopped

Finely grated zest and juice of ½ lemon

Heat oil in a small saucepan over low heat, add ginger, turmeric, garlic and onion and stir for 2 minutes until softened.

Add stock, increase heat to medium-high, and bring to the boil. Allow the broth to bubble for 2–3 minutes, then add a sprinkling of any hardier greens (such as kale or silverbeet) and simmer for another 2–3 minutes until wilted, then remove from heat and stir through any lighter greens (such as spinach or lettuce) and the green parts of the spring onions. Add lemon zest and juice (throw in the squeezed lemon, too), season to taste with salt and freshly ground pepper, and serve immediately.

New-age porridge

Whenever we run workshops talking about the nutritional importance of soaking and sprouting grains and seeds, we always talk about porridge. Prior to learning about wholefoods preparation techniques, we found that when we ate porridge we'd invariably be hungry by mid-morning. The simple change of activating the oats and adding a healthy amount of good fats to the bowl makes it possible to power through to lunch. Here we've also used quinoa, which gives the bowl a nutritional boost. With toasted nuts, seeds and fruit, this porridge is a real winner. Start this recipe the night before.

Makes 2 bowls

1⅓ cups (130 g) organic rolled oats

1¼ cups (250 g) tri-colour quinoa

400 ml (14 fl oz) coconut milk

¼ cup (60 ml) maple syrup, plus extra to serve

Toasted nuts and seeds and fresh fruit, to serve

Soak oats overnight in 4 cups (1 litre) water with a pinch of salt. Drain oats first thing in the morning.

Rinse quinoa well, then drain. Place in a saucepan, cover with fresh water, bring to the boil and cook for 12 minutes, then drain.

Place drained oats and cooked quinoa in a saucepan with 1 cup (250 ml) water and place over medium–high heat, stirring, until bubbling. Reduce heat to low, stir in coconut milk and maple syrup and add water to reach your desired porridge consistency.

Divide porridge between two bowls and top with maple syrup, toasted nuts and seeds, and fresh fruit to serve.

Lentil, lemon and mint soup

The original inspiration for this clean, green soup came from a Nigel Slater recipe, and it's both hearty and cleansing at the same time. We often make it after a big celebration such as Christmas, when we might have an interesting stock left over. This dish also works well with a little pancetta or a ham hock thrown in.

Serves 4

2 tablespoons olive oil

1 onion, finely diced

1 celery stalk, thinly sliced

2 large garlic cloves

Small bunch flat-leaf parsley, finely chopped

1¼ cups (260 g) Puy lentils, soaked overnight and drained

4 cups (1 litre) chicken, duck or turkey stock

1 bay leaf

1 lemon, cut in half, plus lemon wedges to serve

3 handfuls mixed greens (whatever you have on hand; spinach, kale or rocket/arugula), coarsely shredded

1 small bunch mint, leaves picked

Heat oil in a large saucepan over medium heat. Add onion, celery and garlic, and cook, stirring occasionally, for 10 minutes until fragrant and golden. Stir in parsley and lentils, then pour in stock and add bay leaf and half the lemon.

Bring to the boil, skimming any froth that rises to the surface, then reduce heat to low, half-cover with a lid, and simmer gently, stirring occasionally, for 20–30 minutes until the lentils are tender but not collapsing into mush.

Remove lemon and bay leaf, then add shredded greens, half the mint and the juice from the second half of the lemon. Ladle the soup into bowls and garnish with the remaining mint. Serve with lemon wedges.

Cauliflower soup with roast kale and pesto

A simple, classic wintry soup amped up with a swirl of cashew pesto and the crunch of roasted kale.

Serves 4

1 tablespoon olive oil or butter

1 onion, diced

1 celery stalk, thinly sliced

1 leek, white part only, thinly sliced

1 cauliflower, chopped into large florets

5 cups (1.25 litres) chicken or vegetable stock

1 handful herb sprigs (we like a mix of parsley, thyme and rosemary), tied into a bunch with kitchen string

⅓ cup (90 g) pesto (use our Activated cashew pesto recipe on page 233, or whatever you have)

ROAST KALE

½ bunch kale, stalks removed

2 tablespoons olive oil

Preheat oven to 180°C (350°F).

Heat oil or butter in a large saucepan over medium heat, add onion, celery and leek, and cook, stirring occasionally, for 10 minutes until softened. Increase heat to high, add cauliflower, stock and herbs and bring to the boil. Reduce to a simmer and cook for 15 minutes until cauliflower is soft.

Meanwhile, for roast kale, toss kale with oil and 2 teaspoons salt and massage to soften the leaves. Spread on baking trays and roast for 10 minutes or until crisp on one side, then flip leaves over and roast for another 5 minutes or until crisp all over.

Remove herbs from soup, then blend soup until smooth with a stick blender. Season to taste with salt and freshly ground pepper, then transfer to serving bowls and swirl a tablespoon of pesto into each. Tear up kale leaves and nestle on top, then season with a little more salt and pepper to serve.

Roasted roots

At the café we're always making big batches of this dish to use in salads,
and at home we might serve it with roast dinner. It's a very simple
dish but one for which there is a real knack and art to getting right.
Different combinations of root vegetables prepared in this way make an
appearance in a few of our favourite dishes, but cooked as per this recipe
it makes a great complete meal with either some aïoli, pesto or hummus and
a green salad. Clean or peel all vegetables and cut them into pieces so that
they cook evenly. This takes a little consideration to get the sizes just so,
but once you play around enough you will get the idea. Don't worry too
much about the quantities or combinations – just use what you have
and be as liberal with the spices as you like.

Serves 4

2 sweet potatoes (skin on),
    cut into wedges

4 carrots, cut into wedges

1 onion, cut into wedges

2 parsnips, cut into wedges

1 large fennel bulb,
    cut into wedges

1 beetroot (beet), cut
    into wedges

2 tablespoons olive oil

1 teaspoon cumin seeds

1 teaspoon fennel seeds

1 teaspoon thyme leaves

Pesto, aïoli or hummus,
    to serve

Preheat oven to 200°C (400°F). Scatter all veg in a big roasting pan,
making sure that there is enough space between them so they
roast rather than steam. Drizzle liberally with oil, season with
salt and scatter over spices and thyme. Roast for about 45 minutes
to 1 hour, turning halfway through cooking time, until tender and
nicely coloured with caramelised edges. The exact time will
depend on your oven and how big you've cut the vegetables.

Serve hot, at room temperature or from the fridge with aïoli,
pesto or hummus, or use in any of the recipes calling for roast
vegetables in this book.

Golden beets with white-bean hummus

This presents very well as a side dish, but it could equally be the hero in a simple lunch with a good green salad on the side. It's a play on hummus, of course, but we tend to find that white beans often digest a little more easily than chickpeas. You can just as easily use chickpeas, or try it with borlotti beans.

Serves 4–6

1 kg (2 lb 4 oz) golden beetroot (beets; from farmers' markets or select grocers), trimmed, peeled and cut into large bite-sized pieces

100 ml (3½ fl oz) olive oil, plus extra for drizzling

1¼ cups (250 g) dried cannellini beans, soaked in filtered water overnight (or the canned, cooked version if you're short of time)

2 small garlic cloves

2 tablespoons tahini

1 teaspoon ground cumin

Finely grated zest and juice of 1 lemon

Oregano leaves and za'atar, to serve

Preheat oven to 180°C (350°F). Add beetroot to a roasting pan, drizzle with oil and sprinkle with salt. Toss to coat and roast for 40 minutes until just tender and a little caramelised.

Meanwhile, bring a large saucepan of water to the boil. Drain soaked beans, add to saucepan and simmer for 30–40 minutes until very tender. Drain, reserving a quarter of the cooking liquid, and cool briefly.

Add beans to a food processor or blender with garlic, tahini, cumin and a third of the beetroot. Blend, adding oil and some cooking liquid to loosen, until smooth. Season to taste with salt and lemon juice.

Spread white-bean hummus on a platter, top with remaining beetroot, drizzle with oil and sprinkle with lemon zest, oregano leaves and za'atar to serve.

Sashimi with ginger, garlic, tamari and black radish

This dish is built on the premise that the simple things are often the best. If you can get hold of some sustainably caught fish, then even better. This is one of our favourite starters, perfect for a small party of four.

Serves 4

1 tablespoon tamari
1 teaspoon mirin
1 tablespoon olive oil
1 teaspoon sesame oil
Juice of ½ lime
½ garlic clove, finely grated
½ teaspoon finely grated ginger
100 g (3½ oz) sashimi-grade
   kingfish, salmon or tuna,
   thinly sliced across the grain
Radish, cut into matchsticks,
   to serve
Microherbs, to serve

Combine tamari, mirin, olive oil, sesame oil and lime juice in a small bowl with garlic and ginger. Whisk to combine.

Arrange fish beautifully on a platter, drizzle over a little dressing, top with radish and microherbs and finish with remaining dressing to serve.

Quinoa discovery bowl

This recipe is so simple and can be adjusted with any number of seasonal variations. You start with well-seasoned quinoa, mix through some roast, steamed and fresh vegetables and leaves, then top with nuts, seeds and sprouts. To finish, you just need a dressing that brings it all together. The below is a guide; you can explore the potential from here. This happens to be vegan, but you can add any protein you like. Start a day ahead to soak chickpeas.

Serves 2

1 cup (200 g) quinoa

1 garlic clove

3 thyme sprigs, leaves picked

½ cup (65 g) podded peas, fresh or frozen

2 handfuls wild rocket (arugula) leaves

40 g (1½ oz) kale, shredded

2 tablespoons Kombucha vinaigrette (see page 227)

1 avocado, quartered or sliced

2 radishes (try interesting varieties such as black or watermelon), thinly sliced

Edible flowers (optional), to serve

TURMERIC HUMMUS

1¼ cups (250 g) dried chickpeas

2 garlic cloves

20 g (¾ oz) piece fresh turmeric

¼ cup (65 g) tahini

2½ tablespoons olive oil

Juice of 1 lemon

½ teaspoon ground turmeric

For turmeric hummus, place chickpeas in a large bowl, cover with plenty of filtered water and soak for 8 hours or overnight.

Drain and rinse chickpeas, then transfer to a large saucepan, cover well with fresh water and bring to a simmer. Simmer for 30–45 minutes until very soft, topping up water if necessary. Drain, reserving 2½ tablespoons cooking liquid.

Blitz garlic and fresh turmeric in a food processor with reserved cooking liquid, then add chickpeas and remaining ingredients. Blend, loosening with more water if necessary, until mixture is smooth and thick. Season with 2 teaspoons salt.

Place quinoa in a saucepan with garlic and plenty of salted water. Bring to the boil, then reduce heat to low and simmer for 15 minutes or until tender with a little bite remaining. Drain well, return to saucepan, add thyme leaves, then stand for 10 minutes. Fluff with a fork, crushing and mixing through the now soft garlic clove. Cool.

Blanch peas for 1 minute in a saucepan of boiling salted water, then refresh in iced water.

Drain peas and combine with quinoa, rocket and kale. Add half the dressing, toss to coat and season to taste with salt and freshly ground pepper.

Divide hummus among bowls, then heap quinoa mixture on top. Top with avocado and radish, spoon remaining dressing over, and finish with edible flowers, if you like.

Cinnamon-roast pumpkin with charred broccolini and tahini

This dish works as a side but it's also totally able to stand alone as a simple main with a green salad. We like to leave the skin on the pumpkin and the seeds in, which both caramelise nicely when roasted.

Serves 2–4

1 butternut pumpkin (squash), cut into chunks

⅓ cup (80 ml) olive oil

2 cinnamon sticks, broken into 2–3 pieces

1 bunch broccolini or purple sprouting broccoli

1 cup (250 ml) Almond-tahini purée (see page 73)

1 handful coriander (cilantro) leaves

Red-vein sorrel leaves (optional), to serve

1 teaspoon nigella seeds

Preheat oven to 200°C (400°F). Spread pumpkin in a roasting pan, drizzle with half the oil, season with salt, then scatter the cinnamon around. Roast for 30–40 minutes or until tender and caramelised.

Meanwhile, blanch broccolini in a saucepan of boiling salted water for 20 seconds, then drain well. Heat a char-grill pan or barbecue to high, brush broccolini with remaining oil and grill for 2 minutes each side, until nicely charred and tender.

Transfer pumpkin to a plate, top with broccolini and drizzle with almond-tahini purée. Finish with coriander, red-vein sorrel and nigella seeds.

Super slow-cooked lamb stew

This basic cooking method can be used with many different cuts of meat, including shoulder and ribs. The real magic comes from when the tough and sinewy cuts become tender, and if there are bones (particularly marrow bones) in the mix, this dish gains an unctuousness and richness that is deeply satisfying. Since the meat has broken down, it's easy to digest and the gravy will be rich in nutrients, including collagen and gelatine, which help to soothe the digestive system. We love the combination of dried mint, fennel seeds and porcini powder; it gives it an edge that's a bit different. Serve this with baked potatoes or Sprouted buckwheat (see page 66).

Serves 4

2 tablespoons olive oil

4 lamb shanks

1 onion, roughly chopped

2 garlic cloves, chopped

2 carrots, roughly chopped

1 celery stalk, roughly chopped

1 leek (white part only),
   roughly chopped

2 teaspoons fennel seeds

1 teaspoon thyme leaves

1 teaspoon dried mint

1 teaspoon porcini powder

1 swede, roughly chopped

1 turnip, roughly chopped

2 parsnips, roughly chopped

1–2 cups (250–500 ml)
   chicken stock (see page 234),
   to top up

GREMOLATA

3 handfuls chopped mint and
   flat-leaf parsley

1 garlic clove, finely chopped

Finely grated zest of 1 lemon

Preheat oven to 90°C (200°F). Heat oil in a large, ovenproof, heavy-based saucepan (cast-iron is ideal) over medium–high heat until melted and shimmering. Add lamb shanks and fry, turning, for 8–10 minutes until browned all over. Remove lamb and set aside.

Reduce heat to low, add onion and garlic and fry gently, stirring occasionally, for 5 minutes until fragrant and soft. Add carrot, celery and leek, and cook gently for another 5 minutes, then add fennel seeds, thyme, dried mint and porcini powder. Fry, stirring occasionally, for 5 minutes or until aromatic.

Return lamb to the saucepan along with swede, turnip, parsnip and enough stock to just cover. Cover with a circle of baking paper, then a lid, then transfer to oven and cook for 6–8 hours (or overnight) or until meat is falling off the bone. (If you need to speed things up, you can use slightly less stock, whack up the temperature to 180°C/350°F for 30 minutes, then reduce to 150°C/300°F and cook for a further 90 minutes.) Rest for 10 minutes.

Meanwhile, make the gremolata by combining all ingredients in a small bowl.

Serve at the table straight from the pot with gremolata sprinkled liberally over the top.

Slow-cooked pork shoulder

This dish grew from a one-off Father's Day special, going through
several different versions before we landed on the one shown here.
If you like pork, this is a very, very good way to eat it. Ideally you'd have some
BBQ sauce (see page 225) ready to go in the fridge, but if not it copes nicely
with the cooking juices served on the side. We like to accompany it with a sweet
potato and onion hash, some coleslaw, a poached egg and some of our
sauerkraut to aid digestion.

Serves 8

2 kg (4 lb 8 oz) pork shoulder,
  bone in
Olive oil, for drizzling
4 garlic cloves
20 g (¾ oz) fresh turmeric
20 g (¾ oz) ginger
1 tablespoon ground cumin
1½ teaspoons sweet paprika
1 teaspoon rosemary leaves
1 teaspoon oregano leaves
1 carrot, cut into small dice
1 onion, cut into small dice
BBQ sauce (see page 225) and
  Sauerkraut (see page 238),
  to serve

Preheat oven to the hottest setting possible.

Rub pork with enough oil to lightly coat, then sprinkle it evenly
with salt. Place in a roasting pan and roast for 15 minutes. Remove
from oven and reduce temperature to 90°C (200°F).

Add garlic, turmeric, ginger, cumin, paprika, rosemary
and oregano to a food processor and blitz into a paste. Massage
paste over the pork.

Place the diced carrot and onion in the base of the roasting
pan, then place pork on top. Cover pork with baking paper, then
wrap the entire pan tightly in foil. Return pork to oven and roast
for 12–16 hours until it's incredibly tender and falling apart when
poked or pulled with a fork or tongs.

Remove roasting pan from oven and increase heat to 200°C
(400°F). Allow pork to cool briefly. Gently tease off the rind, using
a knife if necessary, and return the rind to the oven on a raised
grill tray. Roast for 10 minutes, then turn over and continue to
roast until you have crisp, golden crackling.

When your crackling is almost done, pull the pork apart
into bite-sized pieces. Mix the pulled pork together with the
vegetables and juices from the roasting pan and serve with BBQ
sauce and sauerkraut.

Slow-cooked BBQ short ribs

The Ultimate BBQ sauce (page 225) that we serve in the café was originally inspired by a recipe in Ferran Adria's *The Family Meal* cookbook, which we love. Here we've used the base of the sauce as the beginnings of the short-rib gravy. Since this dish is very rich, we like to serve it with either a raw salad, simple steamed greens such as bok choy, or both. It's also super-good if you've got a good kimchi or other lacto-fermented pickle that works with the BBQ flavour.

Serves 6–8

2.5 kg (5 lb 8 oz) beef short-ribs, on the bone

2 tablespoons lard, ghee or olive oil

1 tablespoon olive oil

2 onions, sliced

6 garlic cloves, crushed

75 g (2½ oz) ginger, grated

1 celery stalk, finely chopped

1 carrot, finely diced

1 leek (white part only), finely chopped

2 lemongrass stalks (white part only), bruised

2 tablespoons chopped rosemary leaves

2 oranges, peeled and roughly chopped, seeds removed

2 tablespoons molasses

2 tablespoons rapadura sugar

2 tablespoons Dijon mustard

700 ml (24 fl oz) tomato passata (puréed tomatoes)

Steamed greens, to serve

Freshly grated horseradish (optional), to serve

Preheat oven to 90°C (190°F). Season short-ribs liberally with salt and freshly ground pepper. Heat lard in a large, ovenproof, heavy-based saucepan (cast-iron is ideal) over medium–high heat until melted and shimmering. Add short-ribs in batches and fry, turning, for 3–5 minutes until browned all over. Remove from heat.

Heat oil in a separate large saucepan over medium heat. Add onion, garlic and ginger, stir for 5 minutes, then add celery, carrot, leek, lemongrass and rosemary and fry gently, stirring occasionally, for 10–15 minutes until fragrant and soft. Add orange, molasses, sugar and mustard and stir for 1–2 minutes until sugar dissolves. Stir in tomato passata and 1 teaspoon salt, then pour into the other saucepan to just cover the beef (top it up with water if necessary).

Cover with a lid, transfer to oven and cook for 6–8 hours (or overnight) until the meat is falling off the bone at a touch and the sauce is thick and dark (if the sauce hasn't thickened, you can always remove the meat and gently reduce the sauce on the stove).

Serve beef and reduced sauce in a bowl with steamed greens and top with horseradish.

Poached pears with kefir cream and activated seeds

Poached pears are a simple yet satisfying winter dessert. We tend to make larger batches, then store some in jars in the fridge as banked goodness for another lazier time. Paired with the kefir cream and sweet and savoury activated seeds, it becomes a little more interesting and nourishing. You can substitute the kefir cream with yoghurt or soured cream, and the activated seeds for their raw or toasted counterparts, but this is the pure wholefoods version. The sweet seeds of thyme take a day or two to prep but keep for ages. Use as a nibble, in lunchboxes or as a garnish in dishes both sweet and savoury. You can play around with different seeds but the below works as a good base.

Serves 4

4 firm pears (such as beurre
    Bosc), peeled
1 cup (200 g) rapadura sugar
Finely grated zest and juice
    of 1 orange
Finely grated zest and juice
    of 1 lemon
2 cinnamon sticks
2 star anise
160 ml (⅔ cup) kefir cream

SWEET SEEDS OF THYME
1 cup (155 g) pepitas
    (pumpkin seeds)
1 cup (145 g) sunflower seeds
100 g (3½ oz) golden
    (or brown) linseeds
    (flaxseeds)
100 g (3½ oz) chia seeds
100 g (3½ oz) hemp seeds
2 tablespoons thyme leaves
¼ cup (90 g) raw honey
1 tablespoon sea salt

For sweet seeds of thyme, combine all seeds in a bowl, cover with plenty of filtered water and leave to soak for 8 hours to activate.

Drain well, then spread out on a baking tray lined with baking paper. Preheat oven to 70°C (150°F), scatter seeds with thyme and bake, stirring halfway, for 8–10 hours until dried.

Drizzle with honey and sprinkle with salt, mix to coat, then return to oven for 45 minutes to dry a little more. Sweet seeds will keep in an airtight container for 3 months.

Pour 4 cups (1 litre) water into a saucepan just large enough to fit the pears. Place pears in saucepan, then add sugar, orange and lemon zests and juices, cinnamon and star anise. Place over medium heat, bring to a simmer and simmer for about 10 minutes or until a sharp knife can just pierce through to the centre of the fruit.

Remove pears with a slotted spoon and leave until cool enough to handle. Meanwhile, increase heat to high and continue to simmer the cooking liquid until thickened and reduced by about a third.

Halve pears and place two pieces in four bowls on top of a dollop of kefir cream. Spoon over a couple of tablespoons of reduced cooking liquid and sprinkle with sweet seeds of thyme.

Brazil-nut brownie

This brownie is so satisfying and not too sweet. It's an absolute classic.
Start this recipe a day ahead to soak the chia seeds.

Makes 18 pieces

70 g (2½ oz) chia seeds

400 g (14 oz) dark chocolate,
    chopped

400 g (14 oz) coconut oil

1 teaspoon pure vanilla extract

180 g (6 oz) brown rice flour

1 cup (200 g) rapadura sugar

120 g (4¼ oz) raw sugar

½ cup (60 g) raw cacao powder

1⅔ cups (250 g) Brazil nuts,
    toasted and chopped,
    plus extra to serve

The day before you make the brownies, soak the chia seeds in
340 ml (12 fl oz) filtered water. Leave them to form a gel.

The next day, preheat oven to 200°C (400°F), grease a slice
tin and line it with baking paper. Melt chocolate and coconut oil in
a heatproof bowl set over a saucepan of simmering water (don't let
the bowl touch the water). Stir to combine, remove from heat and
add vanilla.

In a separate bowl, whisk together flour, sugars, cacao and
1 teaspoon salt. Add chocolate mixture to the dry ingredients and
stir to form a batter. Stir chia mix through the batter, then fold in
Brazil nuts. Pour batter into prepared tin.

Immediately before placing the brownie in the oven, reduce
the oven temperature to 175°C (325°F); this will help form a nice
crust. Place tin in oven, and bake for 35 minutes until a crust has
formed, the brownie is cooked through and a skewer comes out
mostly clean.

Remove brownie from oven, sprinkle with extra Brazil nuts
and lightly press them into the brownie with a spoon. Allow to cool
in tin, then chill before cutting into 18 pieces.

Choc-chip cookies

Everyone likes a choc-chip cookie. These are pretty shameful, with their only redeeming quality being that we use good unrefined ingredients. Enjoy!

Makes 12

1⅔ cups (220 g) buckwheat flour
1 teaspoon baking powder
170 g (6 oz) unsalted butter
100 g (6½ oz) rapadura sugar
50 g (1¾ oz) raw sugar
1 organic egg, plus 2 organic egg yolks
1 cup (170 g) dark chocolate chips

Preheat oven to 190°C (375°F). Grease two baking trays and line them with baking paper.

Whisk together flour, baking powder and 1 teaspoon salt in a bowl.

Heat a small saucepan over medium heat, add 120 g (4¼ oz) butter and swirl until nut-brown. Remove from heat and cool for 5 minutes, then whisk in remaining 50 g (1¾ oz) butter. Add sugars and whisk to dissolve. Whisk in egg and egg yolks.

Fold dry ingredients through wet ingredients, then fold in chocolate chips. Wrap dough in plastic wrap and chill for 30 minutes to firm up.

Divide dough into 12 equal portions and roll into balls between the palms of your hands. Place on lined trays, press flat, and bake for 8 minutes until spread and set. Remove from oven and cool on tray.

Basic wholefoods

We use these basic preparations throughout the year
as flavourful, nourishing building blocks for our recipes.

Aïoli, page 231

Ultimate BBQ sauce, page 225

Fermented mustard, page 224

Activated cashew
pesto, page 233

Salsa verde, page 233

Slow-fermented tomato chutney, page 226

Cashew cream, page 224

The power of sauce

We love sauces and condiments so much we almost called our original café 'Soul Sauce'. Many of the savoury dishes in this book include sauce, be it a pesto, tomato sauce, mayo, green sauce or a particular salad dressing. With the knowledge of sauces and condiments, you can turn the simplest of foods into great dishes, simply by providing counterpoints in taste and texture or by balancing simplicity with richness.

Fermented mustard

This is our chef Gabe's recipe; it's the best we've ever tasted, with all the nutritional benefits of being homemade and naturally fermented.

Makes 500 g (1 lb 2 oz)

⅔ cup (110 g) each yellow and
  black mustard seeds
300 ml (10½ fl oz) 'vintage'
  kombucha (liquid from
  a jar with a SCOBY)
20 g (¾ oz) nutritional yeast
1 teaspoon ground turmeric
1 teaspoon sweet paprika
1 tablespoon cider vinegar

Grind mustard seeds to a coarse powder in a spice grinder, food processor or a high-speed blender. Transfer to a bowl, add remaining ingredients, except vinegar, then add 3 teaspoons sea salt and stir to combine.

Transfer mixture to a large jar or container, place a piece of muslin over the top and seal it with a rubber band, then leave at room temperature, out of direct sunlight, for 5 days to ferment.

Add vinegar, stir to combine, then transfer mustard to jars and store in the refrigerator. Mustard will keep for 3 months.

Cashew cream

The savoury version of this cream finds its way into a few of our recipes, while the sweet version is a good substitute for a dairy cream.

Makes 2 cups (500 ml)

1½ cups (250 g) raw cashews

FOR A SAVOURY CREAM
1 teaspoon nutritional yeast
1 teaspoon sea salt
1 teaspoon beetroot powder
  (for colour, optional)

FOR A SWEET CREAM
2 tablespoons maple syrup
Pinch of sea salt

Soak cashews in 2 cups (500 ml) cold water overnight. This long, slow soak results in a silkier cashew cream.

In the morning, rinse the nuts well, then place them in a blender with 1 cup (250 ml) fresh cold water and blend until light and creamy. You may have to scrape the mix down with a spatula to help the cream blend evenly. Add either savoury or sweet flavourings and blend well to combine. The cashew cream will keep in the fridge for up to 5 days.

Ultimate BBQ sauce

The original recipe for this came from Ferran Adria's *The Family Meal*, but we've modified it to contain only unrefined sugars. This sauce was the inspiration for our slow-cooked ribs (see page 212): we had ribs on and were prepping this sauce at the same time and a cross-pollination happened – with positive results!

Makes 6 cups (1.5 litres)

2½ tablespoons olive oil

1 kg (2 lb 4 oz) red onions, diced

5 garlic cloves, crushed

65 g (2¼ oz) ginger, grated

1 lemongrass stalk (white part only), finely chopped

1¼ cups (250 g) rapadura sugar

100 ml (3½ fl oz) molasses

75 ml (2¼ fl oz) maple syrup

1 cup (250 ml) freshly squeezed orange juice

100 ml (3½ fl oz) apple cider vinegar

¼ cup (60 g) Dijon mustard

1 tablespoon Worcestershire sauce

1.5 kg (3 lb 5 oz) tomatoes, diced

2 cups (500 ml) tomato passata (puréed tomatoes)

Heat oil in a saucepan over low heat. Add onion, garlic, ginger and lemongrass and cook, stirring occasionally, for 5–10 minutes until soft. Add sugar, molasses and maple syrup, cook gently for another 3–5 minutes, then add orange juice, vinegar, mustard and Worcestershire sauce. Bring to a simmer, then add tomatoes and passata. Bring back to a gentle simmer and cook, stirring occasionally, for 20–30 minutes until sauce has reduced and thickened. Adjust the seasoning to taste, then leave to cool briefly.

Blitz sauce in a food processor or blender until smooth, then store in sterilised glass jars or bottles. BBQ sauce will keep for about 10 days in the fridge or up to a few months in the freezer.

Slow-fermented tomato chutney

Good chutney is a must. There are so many variations that excite us, but this
tomato chutney is the one we return to time and time again. It all comes back
to the same principle: that if you have a few good sauces, chutneys and pickles
knocking about in the fridge or on your counter, you can turn something as
simple as a piece of quality bread, a slice of cheese and a green leaf into a thing
that makes you and your guests happy. The low-quality chutney imitations you
buy from the shops (regardless of how fancy and traditional their labels look)
just don't have the same goodness as those made in your own kitchen.
You'll need three to four 500 ml (17 fl oz) sterilised jars (see page 238).

Makes approximately 6 cups (1.5 litres)

2 teaspoons cumin seeds

1 tablespoon olive oil

2 onions, diced

5 garlic cloves, chopped

3 cm (1¼ in) piece fresh
   turmeric, finely grated

2 teaspoons ground cumin

1 teaspoon rosemary leaves,
   roughly chopped

1 teaspoon thyme leaves

1 kg (2 lb 4 oz) tomatoes, diced

2½ tablespoons raw apple
   cider vinegar

Rapadura sugar, to taste

In a dry pan big enough to hold all ingredients, toast cumin seeds
over medium heat until fragrant. Remove from pan and set aside.

Add oil to pan, followed by onion, garlic and turmeric. Gently
fry, stirring, for 10 minutes until onions are translucent, adding
ground cumin (not toasted seeds) after 2–3 minutes.

Add rosemary and thyme, followed by tomatoes. Season
with a pinch of salt and freshly ground pepper, add toasted cumin
seeds, then bring to the boil. Reduce the heat to low and simmer,
stirring occasionally to prevent catching, for 35–40 minutes until
chutney has thickened and reduced by about a third. Add vinegar
and season to taste, adding sugar to balance the acidity. Transfer
to jars while hot and seal immediately with lids. Store at room
temperature in a cool, dark place.

This chutney will taste good straight away but will also
mature beautifully over a couple of months out of the fridge. The
addition of the raw vinegar and sugar at the end will set up a slow
fermentation to help the chutney develop more flavour and
a sweet-sourness that is different from your standard chutney.
Alternatively, you can keep it in the fridge.

Ghee

Ghee is a clarified butter that is used throughout Asia, particularly in India, where it's revered for its medicinal properties. It has a high smoke point, so it can be used for cooking at high temperatures, and it's super-nutritious and tasty. Whenever we make a batch, we save a little of the warm ghee to make gheeonnaise (see page 70), which is fantastic with baby spring vegetables.

Makes 2 cups (500 ml)

500 g (1 lb 2 oz) unsalted organic butter

Melt butter in a saucepan over low heat. When fully melted and starting to bubble, give it an initial stir. As a crust begins to form on the surface, skim this off.

Keep skimming the crust until the liquid is completely clear, being careful not to let the solids collecting on the bottom burn too much. Strain through paper towel or muslin into a jar, cover and store for a month at room temperature, or in the fridge indefinitely.

Kombucha vinaigrette

This vinaigrette swaps out a standard vinegar with a very sour kombucha. We also add our own house-fermented mustard, which gives it an extra touch of greatness.

Makes approximately ½ cup (125 ml)

⅓ garlic clove, finely grated
1 teaspoon Fermented mustard (see page 224)
2 tablespoons 'vintage' kombucha (liquid from a jar with a SCOBY)
½ cup (125 ml) extra-virgin olive oil

Place all ingredients in a jar, seal and shake vigorously. Season and adjust ingredients to taste, and use with salads.

Mayonnaise, aïoli and variations

Mayonnaise is a beautiful condiment. It's so versatile while also being highly nutritious – if it's made with the right ingredients. The homemade version, using raw organic eggs and good oils, can be an incredible source of healthy fats and protein and thus a real 'super food' that most of us can indulge in as much as we like.

Once you know how to create this sauce, all of a sudden you have something in your fridge that can turn old vegetables – steamed, roasted or fried – into something fun. Or it could be a crisp salad. With mayo, your slaw becomes sexy, plain fish becomes interesting, cold meats rock. The list goes on.

Angus, a good friend of ours, recently told us that we'd ruined his appreciation of shop-bought mayonnaise and that now he could only eat homemade. We said, 'Good! One down, many more millions to go.' You just need to learn to make it, and that's final. The heavens will open.

There are two basic ways to make mayonnaise that we're going to detail here: the more traditional way using a hand whisk, and the far easier method of using a stick blender. Both can be prone to issues, but both will deliver the goods with a bit of practice.

Mayonnaise: the traditional way

Any budding cook needs to learn to make mayonnaise by hand; it's a rite of passage into a higher level of culinary expertise! The trick lies in learning how to blend the protein of the yolk with the fat of the oil to create an emulsion. See this initiation into the art of mayonnaise as an adventure, and as with all meaningful journeys the end result will be worth the trials and tribulations. This is our signature mayo containing a kick of garlic.

Makes 2½ cups (625 ml)

2 organic egg yolks

Splash of apple cider vinegar

1 garlic clove, finely grated or minced

1 teaspoon Dijon mustard (or Fermented mustard, see page 224)

2 cups (500 ml) light-flavoured olive oil

Lemon juice, to taste

Place egg yolks in a clean bowl that will happily sit on your kitchen counter as you go at it with a whisk. A heavier ceramic bowl is best, but if you are using a metal one then it's often useful to roll up a tea towel and circle it around the base of the bowl so it doesn't flip all over the place. You are going to need both hands free: one to drizzle the oil and the other to whisk.

Add vinegar, garlic, mustard and a pinch of salt to egg yolks and whisk to combine. Begin whisking steadily and continue to whisk as you start to slowly drizzle the oil into your egg mixture. Add the oil very slowly at first, in a continuous slow drizzle, making sure to incorporate it well into the egg mixture. The mixture should remain shiny and smooth at all times. If you see any graininess, stop adding the oil and whisk vigorously.

Once you've added about 100 ml (3½ fl oz) oil, if the mixture is looking smooth and is thickening nicely, you can be a bit more blasé with the flow of oil and increase it to a steady stream. If your mixture becomes too thick so that whisking is tricky, add a splash of water to loosen the mix before continuing. When you have the consistency you want, taste and adjust the seasoning with extra salt for body and lemon juice or vinegar for a touch more acid to cut through all the good fats from the oil.

Mayonnaise: the modern way

You can, of course, just skip the rite of passage on page 229 and go straight to this method, which tends to be the way restaurants make mayonnaise. You'll need a good hand-held blender along with the jug that normally comes with it. Whereas with the traditional method you have to nurture the emulsion carefully, the speed of the blades here do the work for you. The only other difference – a vital one – is that here you use a whole egg.

Makes 2½ cups (625 ml)

1 organic egg

Splash of apple cider vinegar

1 teaspoon Dijon mustard (or Fermented mustard, page 224)

1 garlic clove, finely grated

2 cups (500 ml) light-flavoured olive oil

Lemon juice, to taste

Place all ingredients, except oil, in the bottom of a blender jug and add a pinch of salt. Blend until well combined, then keep blending while you start to drizzle in oil. Again, slowly at first but once the mixture has taken, you can pour more steadily. As you pour the oil, lift the hand blender up and down in the jug to ensure it's all mixed together evenly. How this plays out on your kitchen counter will depend on the model of blender and the jug you have!

As with the traditional method, if the mayo gets too thick you can loosen with a splash of water. When you have the consistency you want, taste and adjust the seasoning with extra salt for body and lemon juice or vinegar for a touch more acid to cut through all the good fats from the oil.

Variations

HERBED MAYO

Stir finely chopped flat-leaf parsley, basil, dill, chives, chervil, oregano or any other herb that works with your recipe into the mayonnaise once everything is emulsified.

TARTARE

Mix through finely chopped spring onion (scallion), pickled cucumber and capers for the perfect tartare sauce for fish.

MISO MAYO

We like to simply mix unpasteurised miso through the standard mayo to give it an extra umami hit. Great as a dip for crudités.

AÏOLI

Add an extra minced garlic clove or two (adjust it to taste) for an extra hit of garlic flavour.

TURMERIC AÏOLI

To make the delicious, golden turmeric aïoli that we serve at the café, blitz 20 g (¾ oz) grated fresh turmeric in with the egg, before adding the oil, adding the extra garlic as above.

SAFFRON AÏOLI

This spice has a certain magic and a subtle flavour that helps to turn simple things into dishes with depth. In this book, we use it to accompany our Crab cakes (see page 156), but it would work equally well with other fish dishes or with grilled or poached chicken. Source some good-quality saffron, take a large pinch of the strands and pour 100 ml (3½ fl oz) boiled water over the top. Set aside for a while to steep and cool, then strain off the beautiful yellow/rose-coloured water (keep the strands for potential presentation later on); you can use this as the final loosening water element when making your standard aïoli. You may want to add less garlic to your aïoli so its power doesn't overtake the saffron, but that's up to you.

Green sauces

It's impossible to understate the importance of being able to throw simple sauces like these together. They have the power to transform dishes from mediocre to magic. What's more, they're super-easy, and need very little or no guidance beyond the basic principles, which is to take green herbs and leaves and either mash them with a mortar and pestle, chop them by hand or pulse them in a food processor with garlic, oil and nuts or seeds, along with mustard, vinegar, lemon juice and other seasonings. This will create a pungent, piquant and versatile sauce that can be adjusted with more or less acid, and additions such as capers or nuts, to accompany soups, grilled meats, fish and roasted vegetables. The two sauces here are the ones we turn to most often.

Activated cashew pesto

Makes 1 cup (250 ml)

40 g (¼ cup) cashews, soaked
    overnight in enough water
    to cover
1 bunch basil, leaves picked
1 teaspoon apple cider vinegar
1 teaspoon Dijon mustard
1 teaspoon lemon juice
150 ml (5 fl oz) olive oil
1 garlic clove, crushed

In a food processor, blitz soaked and drained cashews with basil, vinegar, mustard, lemon juice, olive oil and garlic until they are well blended but still have some good texture.

Season to taste with salt and pepper. Pesto will keep refrigerated for 7–10 days, or longer if it's covered with olive oil.

Salsa verde

Makes 1 cup (250 ml)

1 small bunch flat-leaf parsley,
    finely chopped
2 handfuls rocket (arugula),
    finely chopped
1 tablespoon capers
1 tablespoon chopped
    green olives
1 garlic clove, finely chopped
2 teaspoons Dijon mustard
2 anchovies (optional)
100 ml (3 ½ fl oz) olive oil

Add ingredients to a food processor and pulse until combined. You can make the final paste as chunky or smooth as you like. Season to taste with salt and pepper. Salsa verde will keep refrigerated for 3–5 days, covered with olive oil, but it's best eaten immediately.

Roast chicken stock

From a nutritional standpoint, the absence of stock pots in the modern kitchen is a disaster, since stocks contain an array of valuable minerals and gelatinous substances that help nourish us and soothe our digestive systems. From a cultural perspective, this loss of knowledge is a real shame: as we lose our culinary skills, or waste and discard food, we disrespect the environment that nurtured its growth. This simple recipe is a way to reclaim that traditional process of nurturing our bodies and being kind to our planet, as well as providing you with an ingredient to transform your cooking from ordinary to sublime.

When you have chicken stock in the fridge or freezer, you have a sense of being able to rest in the knowledge that you can elevate even the most mundane things to those of wonder and awe. With a well-built stock you can turn vegetables salvaged from the bottom of your fridge into a soup that will touch parts of your soul.

A splash of this magical liquid into the pan after frying, grilling or roasting any kind of meat can elevate you to the status of genius chef for having created a gravy that perfectly pairs with the aforementioned meat. In traditional times, all parts of the animal would have been consumed or used in some way, shape or form. One of the most obvious of these is the simple simmering of the leftover bones that results in a broth to give the family (or village) vital sustenance.

Makes about 8 cups (2 litres)

1 cooked chicken carcass, left over from a roast dinner (pick as much meat off as possible and save it for sandwiches)

1 small onion, roughly chopped

1 carrot, roughly chopped

1 celery stalk, roughly chopped

4 small garlic cloves, chopped

1 thumb-sized piece ginger, roughly chopped

Splash of apple cider vinegar (or a leftover glass of wine)

Add chicken carcass to a large saucepan, along with all other ingredients and a large pinch of salt. Don't be overly concerned about the way they're chopped – they don't need to look pretty for the broth to be beautiful.

Add enough cold water to the saucepan to cover the ingredients (approximately 4 litres/135 fl oz). Bring to the boil, skimming off any scum that rises to the surface. Reduce heat to low and allow the stock to simmer gently for 12–18 hours, topping up water if necessary.

Pour the liquid through a fine sieve or a colander to separate solids from the amber-coloured broth. Stock will keep refrigerated for 7 days or frozen (we do it in small portions) for up to 3 months.

Simple beef stock

If you are lucky enough to be able to source good bones from a pasture-raised animal, then beef broth is another excellent food to have in your fridge or freezer. Beef bones have a very high gelatine and collagen content, meaning the stock is quite rich and wonderful for developing depth of flavour in soups and sauces. Get into it and give it a crack.

Makes about 8 cups (2 litres)

2 kg (4 lb 8 oz) pasture-raised beef bones (including some marrow bones if possible, cut into small sections across the bone; ask your butcher to do this)

2 bay leaves

½ bunch thyme

2 tablespoons olive oil

2 onions, roughly chopped

2 carrots, roughly chopped

1 celery stalk, roughly chopped

½ garlic bulb

Preheat oven to 200°C (400°F). Place bones in a large roasting pan (leaving the marrow bones aside if you have them), add bay and thyme, drizzle with oil, sprinkle with 2 teaspoons salt, then roast for 20 minutes until golden.

Transfer to a large stockpot, add any marrow bones along with onion, carrot, celery, garlic and 2 teaspoons salt. Fill pot with water, place over medium–high heat and bring to a simmer.

Cover pot with a lid, reduce temperature to very low and simmer very gently for 12–18 hours, adding more water if it drops below the bones, until fragrant and rich.

Strain through a fine sieve and store in the fridge. Stock will keep refrigerated for a week, or if it's reduced a little more on the stove, it can be frozen in ice-cube trays for up to 3 months.

Sauerkraut, page 238
and Classic kimchi,
page 239. Left: Simple
beef stock, page 235.

Sauerkraut

This sauerkraut flavoured with caraway seeds is amazing. It's so versatile and we chuck it on lots of dishes to great effect. You'll need a large sterilised jar or two.

Makes approximately 6 cups (1.5 litres)

1 kg (2 lb 4 oz) red cabbage, finely shredded (reserve a large leaf or two to help pack the jars)

1 tablespoon caraway seeds

⅓ cup (80 ml) live whey (from live cultured dairy or split raw dairy) or a 5 g (⅛ oz) sachet starter culture (available from select health-food shops and online) or 1 extra tablespoon sea salt

Add cabbage to a large bowl. Add caraway and 1 tablespoon salt, mix well and leave for 5–10 minutes to allow the salt to start extracting the juice from the cabbage, then either pound cabbage gently with a pestle or simply massage and squeeze it with your hands until the juices are beginning to leach out.

Add whey or starter culture (or extra salt), toss to combine, then pack cabbage into a large wide-mouthed jar, pressing it down firmly so the juices submerge the shredded cabbage. Fold reserved cabbage leaf around the top of the cabbage and press it down once more – this will keep the shredded cabbage submerged. We then normally place something like an egg cup or small bowl on top so that when the lid is closed it keeps everything firmly underwater.

Place jar on a plate and leave at room temperature for 5–7 days. You should see signs of bubbling after 1–2 days. Once this early fermentation has begun, transfer the jar to the fridge or a very cool place under the house (our daughter recently dug a pit in the garden for her first sauerkraut – a proud moment!).

Once opened, sauerkraut will keep for 3 months in the fridge.

Sterilising Jars

The official way of sterilising jars is to wash them well with soapy water, then either place them in the oven at 160°C (315°F) for about 15 minutes, or simmer them in water for 5–10 minutes. Allow them to cool in the oven or in the pan, then remove and fill with whatever you want as soon as possible.

Classic kimchi

If Eastern Europe has sauerkraut, Korea has kimchi. Get the balance right and tweak the level of chilli to what you desire and you've got a brilliant healthy condiment that adds a little fermented fire to any number of dishes. There are endless variations; the following is what we, after plenty of experimentation, have come to enjoy at our cafés. As with all fermentation, weight measures don't have to be precisely followed, but the following is a guide. You'll need a large sterilised jar or two, depending on the size of your cabbage.

Makes approximately 6 cups (1.5 litres)

1.25 kg (2 lb 12 oz) Chinese cabbage (wombok), coarsely shredded (reserve a large leaf or two to help pack the jars)

3⅓ cups (500 g) grated carrot

1⅔ cups (250 g) grated daikon

1 bunch spring onions (scallions), roughly chopped

1 tablespoon unrefined sea salt

5 g (⅛ oz) sachet starter culture (available from select health-food shops and online) or 2 extra tablespoons salt

150 g (5½ oz) garlic cloves, crushed

150 g (5½ oz) ginger, grated

150 g (5½ oz) gochujang (Korean chilli paste)

50 g (1¾ oz) dried powdered seaweed (dashima)

50 g (1¾ oz) dried chilli flakes or gochugaru (Korean chilli flakes), or to taste

20 g (¾ oz) smoked paprika

Combine wombok, carrot, daikon and spring onion in a large bowl, add salt and then massage the mix to help release the juices. If you are using a starter culture add it here, mixed with a little water, or add extra salt.

Add remaining ingredients and mix well with either a wooden spoon or a gloved hand. Pack the vegetable mix into jars, pressing down to push out as much of the oxygen as possible. The vegetables have to be packed down and have liquid above them throughout the whole fermentation process; if you need to add more water to achieve this then do so.

Finally, fold whole cabbage leaves into the top of the jar and use an egg cup or small bowl to help keep them down. Seal lid tightly and leave out of the fridge to ferment for 5–7 days before placing in the fridge where it will continue to ferment slowly.

Kimchi will keep refrigerated for 3 months.

Cabbage and cucumber pickles with seaweed

We do love good-quality sweet-and-sour vinegar pickles, particularly cucumber pickles that go with burgers, cheeses and dishes that benefit from tang (see page 245 for our recipe). But there's something about a traditional, lacto-fermented pickle that really does it for us, and this is a good, healthy version. We've included seaweed in the mix to give it some more depth of flavour and to benefit the digestive system, but you can leave it out. You'll need a large sterilised jar or two (see page 238).

Makes approximately 8 cups (2 litres)

1 kg (2 lb 4 oz) white cabbage, shredded (reserve a large leaf or two to help pack the jars)

1 kg (2 lb 4 oz) Lebanese (short) cucumbers, coarsely grated

2 garlic cloves, crushed

2 teaspoons dill seeds

2 teaspoons fennel seeds

2 teaspoons dulse flakes (from select health-food shops, and Egg of the Universe)

1 tablespoon unrefined sea salt

5 g (⅛ oz) sachet starter culture (available from select health-food shops and online) or 1 extra tablespoon salt

Combine all ingredients in a large bowl and massage gently to draw out the liquid. Pack into jars and press down until the juice rises above the level of the vegetables. Fold the large cabbage leaf over the top of the vegetables, trying to seal them underneath. Use an egg cup or small bowl to help keep them down. Seal the lid tightly and leave out of the fridge to ferment for 5–7 days before placing in the fridge. It will continue to ferment slowly.

Serve wherever you'd serve dill pickles. Pickles will keep refrigerated for at least 3 months.

Pickled cucumbers, page 245

Pickled onions, page 244

Cabbage and cucumber pickles
with seaweed, page 240

Pickled onions

Everyone loves a pickled onion. This is one of the few pickles that we prefer to make with vinegar, rather than lacto-fermenting it. It just ends up being that little bit more satisfying.

Makes 2.5 kg (5 lb 8 oz)

4 star anise
3 teaspoons fennel seeds
3 teaspoons black peppercorns
2 teaspoons juniper berries
2 teaspoons brown
   mustard seeds
1 teaspoon allspice
2 cloves
4 cups (1 litre) apple
   cider vinegar
60 g (2¼ oz) Himalayan
   pink salt
4 bay leaves
1 teaspoon ground ginger
1 teaspoon ground cinnamon
2.5 kg (5 lb 8 oz) small pickling
   onions, topped, tailed
   and peeled

Dry-roast whole spices in a large saucepan, tossing, for 2 minutes or until fragrant. Pour in vinegar and salt and bring to the boil.

Add bay leaves, ginger and cinnamon along with the onions and 4 cups (1 litre) water. Bring to a gentle simmer and simmer for 5 minutes until onions are just past raw.

Remove onions with a slotted spoon and transfer to sterilised jars (see page 238). Pour in the hot pickling liquid, adding more hot water if needed to cover, then seal jars with lids and allow to cool overnight before serving. Pickled onions will keep, unopened in a cool, dark place, for up to a year; refrigerate once opened.

Pickled cucumbers

While we find that more traditional lacto-fermented pickles tend to feel and taste better, there are times this method fails to produce the required flavour and texture because it breaks down the vegetable. Cucumber and vegetables such as cauliflower are in this category, so if you want that pickled cucumber in your burger or picnic lunch, then a vinegar pickle is the only way.

Makes 2.5 kg (5 lb 8 oz)

2.5 kg (5 lb 8 oz) small
kirby cucumbers (pickling
cucumbers; around
15 cm/6 in long)
½ bunch dill
4 star anise
3 teaspoons fennel seeds
3 teaspoons black peppercorns
2 teaspoons Sichuan
peppercorns
2 teaspoons juniper berries
2 teaspoons nigella seeds
4 cups (1 litre) apple
cider vinegar
60 g (2¼ oz) Himalayan
pink salt
4 bay leaves

Wash cucumbers well and drain. Divide cucumbers and dill between as many sterilised jars (see page 238) as required (if your cucumbers are too long they can be cut into appropriate lengths).

Dry-roast spices in a large saucepan over medium–high heat, stirring, until fragrant, about 2 minutes. Add vinegar, salt, bay leaves and 4 cups (1 litre) water, bring to a simmer and simmer for 5 minutes.

Pour hot pickling liquid over cucumbers and dill, filling jars to the top, then screw caps on immediately and allow to sit overnight before serving.

Pickled cucumbers will keep, unopened in a cool, dark place, for up to a year; refrigerate once opened.

Activated crackers

This healthy spiced seed cracker is brilliant with our Perfect circle (see page 109) or any dip, pâté or spread. The key is to soak your seeds thoroughly, then bake them slowly in the oven until they're completely dry and crunchy.

Makes 1 batch

300 g (10½ oz) golden linseeds (flaxseeds)
⅓ cup (55 g) sunflower seeds
⅓ cup (55 g) pepitas (pumpkin seeds)
1.5 kg (3 lb 5 oz) carrot, coarsely grated
1 teaspoon coriander seeds
1 teaspoon cumin seeds
1 teaspoon smoked paprika
2 teaspoons tomato powder (optional; from select health-food shops)
2 tablespoons unrefined sea salt

Combine the linseeds, sunflower seeds and pepitas in a large container, cover with plenty of filtered water and soak for at least 8 hours or overnight.

The next day, drain well and combine with all ingredients. Line three oven trays with baking paper, then divide mixture evenly among trays, spreading evenly to the edges with your hands. Press down gently with a knife to mark out lines where you'll cut the crackers once they're baked – the size and shape is up to you.

Preheat oven to 70°C (150°F). Bake crackers for 12–14 hours until they're bone-dry. Once they're ready they should lift off the tray and break easily along the marked lines. Store in an airtight container in a dry place for 2 weeks.

Coconut dukkah

A flavourful mix of seeds and spices, with toasted coconut giving it a little twist.
Try this with our Heirloom spring carrots (see page 73).

Makes ½ cup (100 g)

2½ tablespoons black
  sesame seeds
2½ tablespoons white
  sesame seeds
1 tablespoon cumin seeds
1 tablespoon coriander seeds
½ teaspoon fenugreek
½ teaspoon nigella seeds
½ teaspoon fennel seeds
1 teaspoon caraway seeds
½ teaspoon black peppercorns
2½ tablespoons desiccated
  coconut

Toast sesame seeds, tossing, in a dry frying pan for 1–2 minutes until golden. Remove from pan and repeat with spices until fragrant. Blitz to a coarse crumble with a spice grinder or pound with a mortar and pestle.

Toast coconut in a dry frying pan for 1–2 minutes until golden, toss with the dukkah and season with 1½ teaspoons salt. Dukkah will keep in an airtight container for 2 weeks.

Strawberry and wattleseed jam

Jam on toast just makes us happy. This basic technique means you can transform excess seasonal fruits into jams and preserves. The simple wholefoods way of doing this is just to ensure you use high-quality seasonal fruit and an unrefined sugar, so that even though you're creating a high-sugar product it still has nutritional integrity. You'll need sterilised jars for this recipe (see page 238).

Makes 12 cups (3 litres)

2 kg (4 lb 8 oz) strawberries, hulled
950 g (2 lb 2 oz) raw sugar
40 g (1½ oz) pectin powder
40 g (1½ oz) ground wattleseed
1 vanilla bean, split, seeds scraped
Juice of ½ lemon

Combine all ingredients in a large saucepan and bring to a gentle simmer over medium heat, mashing and mixing strawberries as it heats up. Simmer for 5 minutes, then turn off heat and pour or ladle into jars with the help of a wide funnel. Seal with lids and allow to cool with the jars standing upside down on their lids. Jam will keep sealed in a cool, dark place for 3 months.

Drinks and tonics

Kombucha

Kombucha is a traditional brew that involves fermenting a sugar-sweetened tea with the use of a SCOBY (symbiotic culture of bacteria and yeast) to create a probiotic tea tonic. Kombucha is a living thing, and there are many ways to make it. We stop the brewing process at the point where the kombucha is nicely sour but then re-blend it with more botanicals and honey or sugar and put it through a second fermentation until there's a balance of sweetness along with the sour. Many people claim kombucha has wide and varied medicinal qualities; others are less certain. We just think it makes us feel great – explore for yourself.

Makes 2.5 litres (88 fl oz)

¼ cup (20 g) tea leaves (black, green or white)

200 g (7 oz) raw sugar

1 kombucha SCOBY (a friend may have one or search online for suppliers that will send you one – you can also check out our website)

½ cup (125 ml) fermented kombucha tea (this can be from your previous batch or a friend's batch – we sell packets too)

6 cups (1.5 litres) apple or other sweet juice (optional)

Bring 8 cups (2 litres) filtered water to the boil in a saucepan, then add tea. Turn off heat and steep for 3–5 minutes. Strain, then add sugar, stirring to dissolve, and cool to room temperature.

Transfer to a 2–3 litre wide-mouthed glass jar. Add a kombucha SCOBY, along with the already-fermented kombucha tea from your previous batch (when you source a SCOBY for the first time it will normally come with some liquid). Don't fill the jar above the neck; the kombucha needs room to grow and bubble.

Cover the mouth of the jar with muslin, securing it with a rubber band. Allow this brew to sit out for at least 2 weeks, during which time you should witness the SCOBY starting to grow to the edges of the jar. It may sink for a while; it should float up eventually or grow a new SCOBY at the top of the brew.

Over the next 2 weeks the sugar will slowly be converted into acid. Start tasting after 5 days just to test that it's beginning to sour. After 10 days, it should be nicely sour with a hint of sweetness.

Decant into a bottle (leaving about a quarter in the jar for your next batch). You can now drink it as is, keeping it in the fridge, or put it through a second fermentation by mixing it roughly 1:1 with a sweet juice (such as apple). Bottle this new batch and leave it at room temperature for a further 3–5 days – it should have a pleasant fizz.

The longer you leave both the first and second fermentation, the more sour the brew will become – but be warned that long second fermentations can lead to exploding bottles, so be sure to release the gas every couple of days.

Water kefir

This sparkling fermented water can almost be thought of as a natural isotonic sports drink – one that modern counterparts would find hard to rival due to its probiotic, lactic acid and enzyme-rich qualities. It's cultured by adding a symbiotic colony of bacteria and yeast in the form of water kefir granules into sweetened water and allowing it to ferment for 1–2 days. After this, it can either be put through a second fermentation (which is what we do at the café) with ginger and lemon, or simply drunk as is. You can use many different fruits and sugars to flavour the drink, so have fun exploring what flavours you like. Once you have the hang of the basic recipe below, experiment with your own concoctions. You'll need a 2.5-litre sealable glass jar.

Makes 2.5 litres (88 fl oz)

⅔ cup (160 g) water kefir granules (we sell kefir granules, as do other specialty suppliers)

100 g (3½ oz) raw sugar

1 tablespoon roughly chopped ginger (optional)

1 tablespoon roughly chopped fresh turmeric (optional)

Add water kefir granules, sugar and 8 cups (2 litres) filtered water to a 2.5-litre (88 fl oz) sealable glass jar and stir well. Seal jar and leave at room temperature for 1–2 days, depending on how warm the ambient temperature is (as with all fermentation, the warmer it is the faster the reactions will occur).

After this time, when you open the jar you should hear a slight hiss as the gas escapes; the gas indicates fermentation is in progress. Taste to check if the drink has reached a pleasant level of sweetness; if you're happy with the flavour, you can then decant the liquid into a jug, pouring it through a fine sieve. It's ready to drink straight away, but you can bottle it with further flavourings for a more interesting sparkling drink. At Egg of the Universe, we generally ferment the liquid a second time by adding ginger and turmeric and fermenting it for another 1–2 days in a strong sealed bottle. Make sure to release the excess gas every day.

Turmeric-ginger brew

This is a brew that can be enjoyed as a drink to start the day, but it really begins to shine when you may have been out a little too much, drinking and eating more than sense would normally condone. If you line up the health benefits of a fresh lemon, turmeric and ginger brew, you could spend the rest of the day thinking about how good you've been to yourself. As a whole this drink is a digestive cleanser, flushing both liver and kidneys, it's anti-inflammatory and it's alkalising. But really, we'd just encourage you to see how it makes you feel. Try it and see! We have this brew daily straight after waking, before our morning cup of tea.

Makes 300 ml (10½ fl oz)

½ teaspoon finely grated
fresh turmeric
½ teaspoon finely
grated ginger
Juice of ½ lemon

Place turmeric and ginger in a mug or heatproof glass, add lemon and a splash of filtered water, then pour in 300 ml (10½ fl oz) fresh boiling filtered water. Steep for 5 minutes, then stir and consume the whole thing, including the ginger and turmeric. Alternatively, you can thinly slice all the ingredients and brew this in a teapot.

Açai-hemp smoothie

Makes 1

1 cup (250 ml) coconut water
1 tablespoon hemp seeds
1 large banana
1 tablespoon açai powder
1 teaspoon lemon juice

Whizz all ingredients in a blender or bullet until smooth.

Açai berry is full of antioxidants, amino acids and essential fatty acids. With banana for energy and hemp seeds, which also contain healthy fats, this refreshing and uplifting smoothie is a great source of protein and vitamin E. Coconut water restores electrolytes and provides essential hydration.

⟩ **GARNISH:** a scattering of hemp seeds.

Clean green smoothie

Makes 1

1 cup (250 ml) coconut water
½ avocado
1 handful spinach (fresh or frozen)
5 cm (2 in) piece cucumber
10 cm (4 in) piece frozen celery stalk
1 tablespoon diatomaceous earth (from select health-food shops)
3 teaspoons lemon juice
1 teaspoon maple syrup

Whizz all ingredients in a blender or bullet until smooth.

Avocado is very high in omega-3 fatty acids, a great fat and a high-density source of energy for the body. Spinach, cucumber and celery restore hydration and contain many different vitamins and minerals. Diatomaceous earth, also known as fossil-shell flour, is both vegan and gluten-free and can be described as a gentle broom for cleaning the gastro-intestinal tract. A low-sugar, detoxifying but soothing smoothie for digestive health.

⟩ **GARNISH:** a line of desiccated coconut.

Berry good smoothie

Makes 1

1 cup (250 ml) almond milk

1⅔ cups (250 g) fresh or
frozen blueberries

1 teaspoon hemp protein
(from health-food shops)

½ teaspoon vanilla essence

½ tablespoon almond butter

Whizz all ingredients in a blender or bullet until smooth.

Blueberries contain powerful antioxidants that target inflammation and free radicals in the body. Hemp protein is a complete protein containing all nine essential amino acids. Almonds boast an array of minerals and vitamins and stabilise blood-sugar levels among many other health benefits – the good fat in almonds promotes the absorption of fat-soluble vitamins such as vitamin K and promotes longer satiety. Start the day on a high with this breakfast smoothie.

☽ **GARNISH:** a sprinkle of hemp seeds.

Daily allstar smoothie

Makes 1

1 cup (250 ml) coconut water

2 cups chopped kale leaves

1 teaspoon mint leaves

¾ cup (75 g) chopped frozen
apple (such as Granny Smith)

½ small lemon, skin and
pith removed

½ frozen Lebanese
(short) cucumber

1 teaspoon chia seeds, soaked
overnight (or for 20 minutes
at a pinch)

1 teaspoon greens powder
(green superfood powder;
from health-food shops)

Whizz all ingredients in a blender or bullet until smooth.

This smoothie superstar acts as breakfast, lunch or dinner and is a great meal-replacement on the go. Green vegetables are rich in phytonutrients, which lower inflammatory activities in the body and in return help prevent disease on a cellular level. Lemon contains vitamin C and aids the absorption of iron, which most green vegetables have plenty of. Mint is known for its refreshing effects on cognitive function and stimulates healthy digestion, while activated chia seeds are rich in protein and omega-3s.

☽ **GARNISH:** a line of chia seeds (soaked or not).

Clockwise, from bottom left: Clean green smoothie, page 258; Banana, goji and kefir booster, page 263; Green choc-chip, page 263; Berry good smoothie, page 259; Acai-hemp smoothie, page 258; Daily allstar smoothie, page 259; Choc-notella, page 262; Mangorama, page 262.

Mangorama

Makes 1

1 cup (250 ml) coconut milk

1½ cups (200 g) chopped
frozen mango

¾ cup (100 g) chopped
frozen banana

¼ teaspoon pure vanilla extract

Whizz all ingredients in a blender or bullet until smooth.

Mango is a great source of vitamin C, pectin and fibre, all of which contribute to skin health, a healthy cholesterol level and good digestion. Bananas are of similar nature while also adding a healthy boost of potassium to the mix. The beta-carotene in mango is important in the prevention of many diseases, while coconut milk contains medium-chain triglycerides, which positively affect metabolism and energy levels and are less likely to be stored as fat in the body. A fruity and satisfying smoothie with a thick texture.

GARNISH: a drizzle of passionfruit pulp around the jar.

Choc-notella

Makes 1

1 cup (250 ml) almond milk

1 large banana (fresh or frozen)

1 tablespoon almond butter

1 teaspoon chia seeds,
soaked overnight
(or for 20 minutes
at a pinch)

2 tablespoons raw
cacao powder

1 teaspoon maple syrup

Whizz all ingredients in a blender or bullet until smooth.

Raw cacao is the highest plant-based source of iron and is a great alternative to regular caffeine as a gentle stimulant. It contains more calcium than cow's milk and 40 times more antioxidants than blueberries. Chia seeds are full of fibre, minerals and trace minerals such as selenium. Together with the cacao they make this drink an antioxidant weapon. Almond milk and butter provide vitamin B2 and mono-unsaturated fat. An energy-boosting smoothie that also feels like a healthy treat.

GARNISH: dusted raw cacao or cacao nibs.

Green choc-chip

Makes 1

1 cup (250 ml) almond milk

1 banana

1 handful kale or other fresh
greens (we like broccoli
or spinach)

1 teaspoon greens powder
(green superfood powder;
from health-food shops)

½ teaspoon mint leaves

1 tablespoon nut butter
of your choice

1 tablespoon raw cacao powder

1 tablespoon hemp seeds

Whizz all ingredients in a blender or bullet until smooth.

This is our go-to smoothie during the winter months. As the cold sets in, our desire for most smoothies just disappears, but this one is served at room temperature. In terms of nutrition, almond milk is a lactose-free milk alternative that's low-carb, contains many minerals and is high in vitamin E. It's also a great source of calcium and is low in saturated fat. Bananas are rich in vitamin B6. Greens powder contains a full spectrum of beneficial and nutrient-dense elements such as chlorophyll sources and trace minerals. Hemp seeds, which also contain healthy fats, are a great source of protein and vitamin E, while raw cacao is the highest plant-based source of iron. The nut butter, meanwhile, is a good source of protein and healthy fats.

⟩ **GARNISH:** raw cacao powder and hemp seeds.

Banana, goji and kefir booster

Makes 1

1 cup (250 ml) cow's-milk kefir
or yoghurt

1 banana

1 medjool date, pitted

1 teaspoon goji berries
(soaked overnight)

1 teaspoon linseeds (flaxseeds;
soaked overnight)

1 teaspoon ground cinnamon

1 teaspoon honey

Whizz all ingredients in a blender or bullet until smooth.

This is good year-round, but in particular is well suited to the cooler months. The milk kefir provides an excellent boost of probiotics and tryptophan for supporting feelings of happiness.

⟩ **GARNISH:** a sprinkle of ground cinnamon.

Berry good smoothie, page 259

Nut milk

Nut milk

Soak 250 g (9 oz) raw nuts in plenty of filtered water with a pinch of salt for 6–8 hours or overnight. Strain, then blend in ratios of 1 part soaked nuts to 4 parts filtered water. Refrigerate for 1 hour to infuse (if you can wait!), then strain through a fine sieve lined with muslin, squeezing out any excess liquid from the nuts. Nut milk will keep, refrigerated, for 2–3 days. Makes 4 cups (1 litre).

Seasonal brew

Makes 1 teapot

3 lemon myrtle leaves

1 sprig lemon-scented tea tree

1 finger lime (fresh or dried),
cut in half lengthways
(alternatively, use lemon)

1 teaspoon river mint (or mint;
dried or fresh)

We like to play around with making herbal teas from herbs and edible plants you can find around the garden or neighbourhood. Since opening our second space in Eveleigh, with the indigenous rooftop farm run by our friends nearby at Jiwah we've had access to some more interesting botanicals. Basic brews made with the likes of lemon, garlic, ginger and thyme have since developed into more interesting blends using dried finger lime, river mint or lemon myrtle. We would simply recommend brewing what you can find and see if it tastes and feels good. This is an Australian native botanical brew.

Combine all ingredients in a teapot or saucepan and fill with boiling filtered water. Steep for at least 5 minutes before straining into cups.

Brazil-nut matcha bowl

Makes 1

¾ cup (180 ml) Brazil-nut milk
(see page 265)

1 teaspoon matcha powder

2 tablespoons 80°C
(175°F) filtered water

Stevia or maple syrup, to taste

Gently heat Brazil-nut milk in a small saucepan over low heat to just below simmering (be careful not to overheat or it'll split). Meanwhile, in your drinking receptacle of choice – be that a Japanese tea bowl or tea mug (whichever makes you happy) – mix the matcha powder with the hot water, whisking to incorporate. Add the warmed nut milk and sweeten it, if you like, with either stevia or maple syrup.

The coffee butter bullet

Makes 1

150 ml (5 fl oz) fresh-brewed
  black coffee (however you
  like it)
1 teaspoon MCT oil (from
  health-food shops)
1 teaspoon cultured
  unsalted butter

At home we make coffee with an Aeropress, which basically makes a good strong coffee without burning it like the stovetop coffee makers can. We use this as the base for a bullet coffee, a concept made famous by David Asprey in his book *Head Strong*. This is our less fussy version, but the basic concept is that by blending the coffee with fats, the caffeine is more steadily absorbed into the bloodstream. This is by far our favourite way to have coffee and we normally start the day with one.

Combine ingredients in a blender (or in a jug and use a stick blender) and blend together for 15–20 seconds.

Iced mushroom cacao

Makes 1

1 cup (250 ml) coconut milk
1 heaped tablespoon
  ceremonial-grade raw
  cacao powder (from select
  health-food shops)
½ teaspoon MCT oil (from
  health-food shops)
1 tablespoon powdered
  collagen (from select
  health-food shops)
¼ teaspoon medicinal
  mushroom mix (we use
  Mason's Mushrooms,
  available online)
Toasted coconut chips, to serve

Place all ingredients into a blender and blitz until smooth and frothy. Pour over ice and garnish with toasted coconut chips.

Seasonal brew, page 266

Brazil-nut matcha bowl,
page 266

Iced mushroom cacao, page 267

The coffee butter bullet, page 267

Medicinal mushroom hot chocolate

Go-dandy

Medicinal mushroom hot chocolate

Makes 1

1 tablespoon ceremonial-grade
raw cacao powder (from
select health-food shops)
¼ teaspoon medicinal
mushroom mix (we use
Mason's Mushrooms,
available online)
1 tablespoon gelatine powder
½ teaspoons MCT oil (from
health-food shops)
⅔ cup (170 ml) nut milk
(see page 265)

Medicinal mushrooms are prized in many cultures for their ability to build immunity, boost energy, support the nervous system and as potent adaptogens within the body to boost vitality, clarity of mind and longevity.

Combine cacao, mushroom mix, gelatine powder and MCT oil, add a splash of boiling filtered water and stir to make a paste. If it's too thick, add a little more water. Transfer to a small saucepan, add the nut milk and whisk together while heating to your desired temperature. Serve in a mug or cup.

Go-dandy

Makes 1

200 ml (7 fl oz) almond milk
1 teaspoon roasted
dandelion root
½ teaspoon MCT oil (from
health-food shops)
1 teaspoon goji berries
(soaked overnight)

Roasted dandelion root is a good coffee alternative. Once or twice a year when Harry weans himself off coffee, dandelion is the most likely substitute. Not only is it a good liver cleanser, it's also a diuretic, so during spring and autumn it's good as a detoxifying drink. If you get a quality roasted root it's nice as a black tea, but the Go-dandy was developed to be more satisfying, with nut milk, goji berries and MCT oil helping it pack a heftier nutritional punch.

Gently heat almond milk in a saucepan over medium heat. Meanwhile, brew dandelion with a splash of boiling filtered water, leave for 3–5 minutes, then strain into milk. Add MCT oil and goji berries, then blend briefly. Serve in a mug or cup.

Cold-pressed ginger and turmeric shot with grapefruit and orange

200 g (7 oz) ginger, peeled
100 g (3½ oz) fresh
   turmeric, peeled
2 oranges, peeled
1 small or ½ large
   grapefruit, peeled
Pinch cayenne pepper
   (optional)

Ginger is a pretty amazing food, not only for its flavour but also for the benefits it brings to a wide variety of tonics and pick-me-ups. It has been used for millennia for various minor ailments such as nausea, and is thought to help fire up the digestive system by helping to clear the stomach and stimulate gastric-acid production. Turmeric, meanwhile, is considered to be an anti-inflammatory food with a raft of other benefits. This tonic is great as an anti-inflammatory and anti-viral, with a cayenne-pepper hit to clear the nasal passages. It's part of our daily routine during colder months.

Ideally in a cold-press juicer (or regular one if that's what you have), juice all the roots and fruits, allowing everything to mix well. Taste and add extra sweet juice from an additional orange, if necessary. Add a small pinch of cayenne, mix and taste to see if you would like any more. Drink in one quick shot.

Apple cider vinegar shot

Makes 1

30 ml (1 fl oz) live apple
   cider vinegar

Again, this has been used to fire up the digestive system for many years. We've used it if our digestion is sluggish and as an aid for liver and gall-bladder cleansing. It's also been suggested that the malic acid in apple cider vinegar can help cleanse the pineal gland of toxins. For this, you'll need to buy a live vinegar with the mother. We normally have a shot before eating if our digestion is slow, or first thing in the morning if we've run out of lemons for our hot lemon morning brew.

Pour out a shot of live apple cider vinegar and drink before breakfast, or at least on an empty stomach. You can also dilute it in a glass of water.

Wheatgrass shots

Makes 1

30 ml (1 fl oz) wheatgrass juice

If we can get hold of fresh wheatgrass then we'll juice this instead of having the commercial chlorophyll. It has a deep cooling sense about it, so if you already have a slow digestive system, see how this feels and use a different supplement. We love this during the hotter months of the year.

Pour out a shot of juice and drink before breakfast, or at least on an empty stomach.

Fire tonic

Makes 2 litres (67 fl oz)

1 onion, chopped
1 small carrot, peeled, trimmed
   and thinly sliced
2 jalapeños, chopped
10 garlic cloves, chopped
¼ cup (30 g) grated ginger
¼ cup (30 g) grated horseradish
   root (fresh or dried)
1 tablespoon grated turmeric
1 orange, peeled and chopped
2 tablespoons chopped rosemary
1 teaspoon brown mustard seeds
1 teaspoon black peppercorns
4 star anise
Peeled zest and juice of 1 lemon
¼ cup (60 ml) organic honey
   or maple syrup
1 cup (250 ml) organic apple
   cider vinegar

Have this tonic anytime you feel that your digestive system needs a little perk up or if you feel immune-compromised or just run down. The elements within have good antimicrobial, anti-inflammatory, immune-boosting properties – it tastes alive. You can adjust the amount of fire by changing the type of chilli you include – play around and see what you like.

Combine all ingredients, except vinegar, in a metal bowl with a pinch of salt, then pound gently with a pestle or wooden rolling pin to release all the flavour. Transfer to a 2-litre jar, add vinegar, top up with filtered water so the jar is full, then seal.

Leave for 10–14 days and you'll have a good brew, but feel free to taste along the way or leave for longer. You can then decant the brew into bottles that will happily sit in the fridge.

From left: Water kefir, page 255;
Kombucha SCOBY; Sweet tea brew for
kombucha; Wheatgrass shot, page 273;
pineapple-flavoured kombucha; Ginger and
turmeric shot, page 272; Kombucha, page 252.

Acknowledgements

There are many people we would like to thank for bringing this book into being. Firstly, to Kelly Doust, who after knowing of us for many years as a student offered to publish the book for us. Thank you for your endless support and faith.

To all the people at Murdoch Books who stood behind that decision and brought the best out of us, thank you for your patience as we grappled with opening our second space and the challenges of a global pandemic. To Sarah Odgers for the beautiful design, David Matthews for the edits, Megan Pigott for heading up creative, Sarah Hatton for helping us share it with the world and Virginia Birch for pulling it all together with such grace. Thank you, and everyone there – what a privilege it's been to work with such a wonderful publishing house.

We are surrounded by amazing people, and this book couldn't have been completed without the extraordinary support of all those we've worked with, both past and present and through all the evolutions of our business. In particular our manager, Amy Truslove, who holds the yoga studios with such competence and love, and Belinda Harrold who lifts us up and offers so much in wonderful ways. And to everyone at Egg: our amazing team of teachers, desk angels and karma cleaners, who all contribute to making the studios feel so warm and special – a tapestry of wonderful souls.

To our café team of chefs, managers, kitchen hands, baristas and service staff who do the hard work of pulling together to create great food and serve our community. Many of our key chefs and managers have collectively helped evolve the menus and recipes in this book. In particular we'd like to thank Svenja Pampel for her great smoothies, and Gabe Hair for many of his amazing cakes and other wonderful elements in this book. Thank you also for your help through the photoshoot. To everyone else we have had the pleasure of working alongside, thank you for helping to deliver our vision to the world.

To Alan Benson, our photographer, who was a complete joy to work alongside, thank you for bringing such beautiful art to each photo. And thank you to Vanessa Austin, who helped bring beauty to every food shot, and to Lara Zilibowitz, who provided the illustrations, bringing a whimsical personality to the pages – thank you for imbuing them with such love.

To Craig New, Katie Rose and Ally McManus, thank you for your early read-throughs and support. And to Jennifer Richards, for helping to pull some recipes together during the most challenging of times.

To both sets of our parents – Helen and Richard Lancaster in England and Jane and Jonathan King in Sydney – thank you for your endless support of us, our vision and our life together working to bring Egg into fruition. To our patient friends and family from whom we've been rather absent as we've beavered away at building our new sites and writing this book – thank you for your love, laughter and encouragement.

Deep bows of respect and gratitude to Kylie Kwong for your support as a friend and inspiration as a leader in all things food and community, and for so generously supporting this book.

We also say thank you to our many teachers, who over many years in yoga and food have so clearly shown the path for us to travel. In particular, we'd like to acknowledge Sarah Powers and Kevin Farrow as teachers of yoga, meditation and energetics, and Sally Fallon and Charles Eisenstein for paving such an inspirational path to follow into wholefoods and the yoga of eating.

To Olive and Leo, thank you for your gentleness and understanding – the lines between our work life and family life can become pretty fluid sometimes. Thank you for both being such wonderful kids, so full of life and so inspiring for us to leave the world a little better than how we found it, and for bringing so much adventure and fun to life. We love you.

And for every person who has ever come to class, bought a pass, taken a workshop, stayed for lunch, enjoyed a chai or supported us in any way! Everyone who is involved with Egg, in the tapestry that is our community, you are all so important to us. Without you, Egg wouldn't be the same. It's such a special place for us and something that supports us as much as we support it. It's a dance of reciprocity and one we hope to continue for many moons to come.

Index

Published in 2021 by Murdoch Books, an imprint of Allen & Unwin

Murdoch Books Australia
83 Alexander Street
Crows Nest NSW 2065
Phone: +61 (0)2 8425 0100
murdochbooks.com.au
info@murdochbooks.com.au

Murdoch Books UK
Ormond House
26–27 Boswell Street
London WC1N 3JZ
Phone: +44 (0) 20 8785 5995
murdochbooks.co.uk
info@murdochbooks.co.uk

For corporate orders and custom publishing,
contact our business development team at
salesenquiries@murdochbooks.com.au

Publisher: Kelly Doust
Editorial Manager: Virginia Birch
Design Manager: Megan Pigott
Editor: David Matthews
Designer: Sarah Odgers
Cover designer: Trisha Garner
Illustrator: Lara Zilibowitz
Photographer: Alan Benson
Stylist: Vanessa Austin
Production Director: Lou Playfair

Text © Bryony and Harry Lancaster 2021
The moral right of the author has been asserted.
Design © Murdoch Books 2021
Photography © Alan Benson 2021
Illustrations © Lara Zilibowitz 2021

Thanks to Splendid Wren Ceramics for supplying
props for the photoshoot.

The Gratitude Quote by Melody Beattie on page 101
reproduced with permission from *The Language of
Letting Go: Hazelden Meditation Series*, Hazelden
Publishing, Minnesota, 1990.

Jon Kabat-Zinn quote on page 42 from zenthinking.net

Every reasonable effort has been made to trace the
owners of copyright materials in this book, but in some
instances this has proven impossible. The author(s) and
publisher will be glad to receive information leading to
more complete acknowledgements in subsequent
printings of the book and in the meantime extend their
apologies for any omissions.

ISBN 978 1 76052 424 1 Australia
ISBN 978 1 91163 212 2 UK

A catalogue record for this book is
available from the National Library
of Australia

A catalogue record for this book is available
from the British Library

Colour reproduction by Splitting Image Colour Studio
Pty Ltd, Clayton, Victoria
Printed by C&C Offset Printing Co. Ltd., China

OVEN GUIDE: You may find cooking times vary
depending on the oven you are using. For fan-forced
ovens, as a general rule, set the oven temperature to
20°C (70°F) lower than indicated in the recipe.

TABLESPOON MEASURES: We have used 20 ml
(4 teaspoon) tablespoon measures. If you are using
a 15 ml (3 teaspoon) tablespoon add an extra teaspoon
of the ingredient for each tablespoon specified.

10 9 8 7 6 5 4 3 2 1